MW01295793

'TIL DEATH DO US PART---AND THEN WHAT?

Have Those Conversations *Now* That Will Prepare Your Spouse to Live On Without You

KAREN R. POST

Copyright © 2013 Karen Post
All rights reserved.

Grateful acknowledgment is given to the distinguished authors on whom I have relied for their knowledge and insight into the areas of the subject matter. Resources are recognized in the footnotes and in the Bibliography.

No part of this book may be reproduced in any form whatsoever, except in the case of brief quotations, without prior written permission of the publisher.

This publication is designed to provide accurate and authoritative information in regard to the subject matter covered. It is sold with the understanding that the author is not engaged in rendering legal, accounting or other professional services. If professional advice or other expert assistance is required, the services of a competent professional person should be sought.

THE PUBLISHING POST
4171 South 620 East
Bldg. 09C – Unit 46
Salt Lake City, UT 84107

thepublishingpost@comcast.net

ISBN - 13:978-1490575452

I dedicate this book to Lynne, David,
Valerie and Thuy….
who were there.

ACKNOWLEDGMENTS

The writing of this book has taken almost 15 very sporadic years. I have probably forgotten many folks from whom I gleaned information in those early years, and to you, I am sorry. But I do owe a debt of gratitude to many, many good friends and family.

The largest group I would recognize as a whole (because they would be too numerous to mention individually) would be all the new widows and widowers who answered my questions, many of them while they were still in the grieving process. A huge thanks to all of them. Specifically I would say thank you to Twila Norton, Coral Paladino, Bruce Pyeatte, and Brent Stratton.

There were those areas, especially in the legal field where I needed specific and accurate information (especially from state to state), so I leaned on the professionals. These included: Burt Cassity, Daniel Gomez, Jim Morgan, David Ranks, Gary Russon, Bob Stayner, Shaida Trebreza, and Robert Whitesides.

For content and editorial help, a big round of applause goes to Ginny and John Hamilton, Deborah Long, Jim McCall, Megan Mullineaux, Linda Newell, Scott Olson, Jim and Bonita Robertson, Don Shrum, Ralph Tamper and Barbara Wheeler.

And for the family perspective, thank you to my two lovely daughters, Lynne Nilson and Valerie Billmire. They were there during those two deteriorating years, especially the last disintegrating two weeks. They have read the drafts and reminded me of things forgotten. David and Thuy, my two other children, and all the wide-ranging grandchildren, who were little then and are big now, complete the story.

Thank you to anyone I may have forgotten and to everyone I have remembered.

KRP

TABLE OF CONTENTS

PROLOGUE

ELEPHANT IN THE ROOM

The day Gary came home and told me he was dying, we had been married 39 years. I suppose they had been married years like most other people's married years--years of passionate, devoted love, and years that were, sometimes, one phone call away from a divorce attorney.

We had been married in the era (late 1950s) when the accepted norm of a marriage was that the housewife stayed home all day, doing her housework while dressed in heels and a crisply ironed dress that had a full bouffant skirt, and the husband left each morning in a suit and tie, carrying his briefcase and headed for the office where he went to "bring home the bacon" for his family. Yeah, right....!

Gary and I were far from the norm. When we were first married, we were both professional musicians playing in the Utah Symphony. Gary was also working at another job, and we were both trying to finish our bachelor degrees. We started out with stress in our marriage, which was soon exacerbated with my first pregnancy. Something had to give--which was my schooling.

By the time our beautiful, little Lynne was born, Gary had graduated and had a full-time job teaching in a high school. I went back to school, but with motherhood and being a full-time musician (Gary was also still playing--full-time), it took me three more years to finish my degree in art and music. When I marched in the graduation procession, I was seven months pregnant with our son, David, but Gary would always say that I didn't look any different from all the others in my balloony black gown.

Valerie followed two years later, and our "normal" married life was playing out. I was trying to bring in extra money with some artwork during the day. Gary would dash home from school at dinner time, we would eat frantically then race off for a symphony rehearsal or concert. We were also actively involved in our church, each of us holding positions that required time and energy.

To illustrate how hectic our lives had become, I got a phone call from an anonymous female one day asking me if I knew that my husband was having an affair. I started laughing and told her if he could find time for an affair in the frantic schedule that he lived, more power to him. I never heard any more from her.

We never took time to just sit and talk with each other. There was always something demanding our attention and whatever that was, it was not to each other. Sometimes it seemed as though just one more thing would be the tipping point to destroying our marriage. Our lives were getting so encumbered and complicated with outside influences, divorce was on our minds more often than not.

But in our culture and time, even thinking about getting a divorce was a sign of weakness and failure. Divorce certainly did happen, and when it did, it brought shame to everyone involved, including the couple's family. Parents of the unhappy couple were particularly humiliated, as though the divorce had been caused by a lack of adequate upbringing. Divorce carried a social stigma.

In addition, Gary and I had been married in a church ceremony where we had declared our devotion to each other for not only our lives here on earth, but for into all eternity. It was a commitment that neither of us took lightly, even though it was becoming more and more difficult.

But we continued to slog through our life together. We had three children and a foster daughter we were raising, all to whom we were both deeply devoted. We had a mortgage, car and boat payments, credit card payments, and other monthly financial debts. We shared good friends and good times, but we just weren't happy with each other.

Our life evolved in and out of different jobs, homes and friends. We certainly didn't hate each other. We did love each other, as you love someone with whom you have shared your life for 39 years. We just didn't love each other anymore in "that" way.

Then came the bomb--the news that Gary was dying. And all of a sudden life snapped into perspective. That which you know you are going to lose, suddenly has great value. My husband was dying. My husband was DYING!

When faced with news like this two things rush into your brain: What about him? What about ME?

THE BEGINNING

I don't know what I was cooking when Gary walked through the door that fall night in 1996 looking ashen and extremely pale. Without even saying "hi" to me, the first words he said were, "I have been to the doctor and he thinks I have a terminal illness."

My mind is a blank as to what happened after that, but it must have been pretty dramatic because I remember that the meat burned. What do you say? How do you respond when your spouse tells you he might be dying? And more than that, I discovered that he had been visiting the doctor for quite a while before he decided to include me in what he was facing.

3

I have always kept a diary of one sort or another, and these are some of the things I recorded of our journey that began that day and lasted for two and a half years:

Sept 5/96   Gary had a CT scan a couple of weeks ago—they have discovered "scarring" in his lungs. They compared the scan with one taken three years ago when he had the liver problem—the lungs are getting progressively worse. They don't know why.

Oct 22/96   We met with Gary's doctor (lungs) yesterday. I guess it's taken until today for it to seep in. Gary has big problems – Idiopathic Pulmonary Fibrosis (IPF). And they have no clue what is causing this very significant scarring in two major organs (also cirrhosis of the liver). The course of action seems to be Prednisone—which will stop the scarring (hopefully), but it has extremely serious side effects. His blood sugar is already high—this could kick him into diabetes. He will have muscle and bone loss. He could develop cataracts. His blood pressure could increase (fortunately it's <u>really</u> low – yesterday it was 102/58). He will probably gain weight – he has been losing recently – yesterday he was 202 lbs. Even though everything points to the contrary (about 25 different blood tests, all which were non-conclusive), it could be a virus. If it is, the Prednisone treatment could be disastrous! Even deadly! The only way to know for sure is to do a biopsy. The doctor can do one through the trachea, but his platelets are so low, if he started to bleed he might not stop. They can do one through the rib cage with laparoscopy – if he bleeds then they can see it. But that's very painful and a 4-5 day hospital stay. Gary is struggling with deciding what to do.

The doctor explained to us that the laparoscopic test was a very extreme test where they would break a rib, go into the lung from his side, collapse the lung and take a biopsy. Without those results, the doctor couldn't be *positively* sure Gary had this horrible, devastating disease. Even so, the doctor was pretty sure he did have IPF, which is a terminal autoimmune disease.

Dec 15/96 Gary sees the doctor tomorrow to decide what his treatment will be. A couple of weeks ago he had his lungs "flushed" so they could collect some matter and do a culture. They also went down for a "look-see." Didn't find anything they didn't already know.

About three years prior to this latest discovery, Gary had been in the Intensive Care Unit with massive internal bleeding. The tests revealed that he had portal hypertension or, a blockage going into the liver. The blood ended up traveling to the heart via veins in the esophagus (varices) which ruptured, causing the internal hemorrhaging.

The doctors got the liver problem under control with medication, but here, now, was scarring of another major organ. These were both autoimmune diseases, but what was causing them? Gary often complained that he had never had the fun of smoking or drinking, and now he had all the end results.

Little by little as the IPF progressed, Gary's stamina began to wane, and he was put on oxygen and Prednisone (I've always said that Prednisone is a wonder drug if it doesn't kill you first). We talked about the illness, but we didn't *ever* discuss the finality of the disease and that I would ultimately be left alone.

I had never known anyone in my personal circle of acquaintances who had taken care of a terminally ill spouse or relative. At the time Gary certainly didn't seem that ill to me, and it was hard for me to even imagine what was in store for me. Well, I thought, I'll cross that bridge when I come to it.

Psychologists tell us that the first stages of grief are disbelief and denial. And that's exactly where both of us went; we simply pretended that nothing was happening. Life went on as it always had—Gary was going to work every day, as was I. We came home and watched TV or went to the movies or went to see our grandchildren. As a ham radio operator, Gary spent many hours in the basement, and I was usually in my sewing room. As always during our marriage, we didn't communicate.

There was a big, fat, unwelcome and unbidden gray elephant that had appeared in our living room. Neither of us wanted to talk about

5

it. I suppose we thought that if we ignored it, either it wasn't there or it would go away without our having to acknowledge its presence. Its color was slowly turning from dark gray to a light pink, and we still didn't want to admit that it was there nor to discuss what its existence meant.

We didn't talk about the deep, emotional and heart-rending situation of his pending death. We didn't talk about me, and what I would be facing—emotionally, financially and practically.

With day after day filled with opportunities for us to become closer, to prepare for the future (both immediate and long-term), to position me in a firmer place as a single person, our default choice was to do-- nothing.

Jan 12/97 Gary is a new man! He started on Prednisone two days before Christmas and on oxygen a few days after. He is pepped up, hyperactive and ready to go. He is only on oxygen at night, so far, but I know this is the beginning of a long haul.

For about two months he ran up the stairs, he walked at a brisk pace, and he was happy. This Gary I hadn't seen for a long time, and I was having a hard time keeping up with him. It was impossible to think that he was ill--much less terminally ill.

After his brief spurt of energy, he started to wind down again. But he was solid, went to work every day, and carried on as normal. He was actually quite viable for about two years--just getting more and more tired as the months went on. He started using more oxygen during the day.

In order to get positioned better, we sold our house and moved into a condominium the summer of 1997. We did a lot of remodeling and redecorating, updating our unit from the 1972 original homeowner's style. Gary did a lot of hefting and lifting, putting in new kitchen and bathroom cabinets, lifting boxes and moving furniture. He had a portable oxygen pack that he carried over his shoulder to give him a boost when he needed it, and he took a lot of naps.

Our kids were an active presence in helping with the remodeling and moving. Without my actually realizing it, they were gradually weaving themselves back into our lives.

Both Lynne and Valerie had new babies--Lynne's Hailey had been born in February, and Val's Ethan the previous November. The two babies were originally supposed to have been born within a few weeks of each other, but Ethan had come too early, at 27 weeks gestation. Even though they were both only months old, the difference in the developmental processes between the two was beginning to be evident.

Our happy little Ethan, though wiggly and smilingly responsive, was just not keeping up with his cousin who was, by now, sitting up and rolling over. Gary began to form a very touching bond with his little grandson. Ethan seemed to sense the frailties of his grandpa, and the two of them formed a tender attachment.

So we were now in our new condominium with all new kitchen and bathrooms, new carpeting and draperies, everything all fresh and new. And now what?

Whenever I had thought about being alone and what it would mean, I thought about my capabilities. First and foremost I had a good job. I understood finances and legal issues pretty well, I had pumped my own gas for years, Gary and I had built a cabin together and I could operate almost any small piece of electrical equipment, I could paint and paper a room like a pro. At this time in my life, there were very few problems that I couldn't work my way out of (or so I thought). If I was going to have to, I figured that I could in all likelihood get along pretty well as a single person.

Finally Gary quit his job, was on full-time oxygen, and the elephant had turned to a bright pink. We still ignored its presence and did not discuss what the realities of my life would be after he was gone. I know, now, that both of us were still at that "denial" phase where we thought that medicine and good care would prolong his life for quite a while longer. We could talk about those things--later. We had plenty of time.

THE ENDING

Then it happened--faster than either of us thought it would. By the time we both began to believe and accept the inevitable, Gary was too ill for us to discuss really what was going to happen to me after he was gone. All we talked about now were the specific end-of-life issues that he wanted to have happen: funeral plans, talking individually with each of the kids and the grandkids, calling old friends, talking about good--and bad--things that needed to be resolved. He accomplished all that, and then he was gone--on a cold, snowy Tuesday in March.

The funeral was over. I pulled into the garage. The back of my car was filled with plants and flowers from Gary's gravesite that could be salvaged for a few days from the freezing cold weather.

I was alone. The past several days had been unrelenting chaos filled with family, friends, relatives, morticians, funeral plans, phone calls, flowers, cards, and more flowers and more cards. I hadn't consciously realized what was happening at the time, but the last few days before Gary died, and until I was pulling into the garage that day, the girls had been rotating their family's schedules so there was someone with me around the clock.

But now everything was over and *I was truly alone*. As the garage door went down behind me, I sat in the car and sobbed. My "aloneness" was now a reality. I was going to walk into that back door, and I was forever more going to be alone. Gary was no longer there, the kids were no longer there, and friends were no longer there. The end had truly come. Life would change--life *had* changed.

I carried the flowers in and lined them up on the dining-room table. For many months my thoughts had been consumed with the here and now, and suddenly I realized that for the immediate future, I needed to start giving serious thought to what my life alone would really be.

It wasn't that I hadn't thought about it before--of course I had. From the very day that Gary told me he was dying, I must admit that one of the major things I kept thinking about was--what about me? I had been married for more years than I had been single. What was that going to mean for me?

I sat down at the table to think. It had been a good funeral. Tomorrow I would clean out the back bedroom of all the medical equipment. After that I would empty the closets and drawers of Gary's clothing and personal effects. Then in a few days I really should get back to work--I had been able to take family medical leave since the beginning of the year.

I clipped the funeral flowers, put them in vases and set the vases around the house where I could see them. I cleaned out the refrigerator of the aging food that had been brought in the past few days--oh, so many casseroles. Enough food to, as they say, feed an army.

But there wasn't an army any more--there was just me. I looked in the living room, even the elephant was gone. Life was going to go on, and I was going to go on with it. I had no idea what was on the horizon waiting for me. All I did know was that the casseroles were going to stop coming. Now I was going to discover what I was *really* in for.

FAST-FORWARD

Two or three months had gone by since the funeral. I had cleaned out the sick room and converted it into my new office, I was paying the monthly bills and seemed to have enough money, I was filling the

9

gas tank, buying the groceries, and I was back at work. Other than being horribly lonely, I was building a new--and different--kind of life to be lived.

One weekend I flushed the toilet and it began to flood over. I grabbed the plunger and plunged. Nothing worked. Water was pouring all over the floor. I grabbed nearby towels while pulling off the tank top. Holding up the floater and sopping up the water, I tried to turn the faucet at the bottom of the toilet. It was corroded solid and wouldn't budge.

I stood there in the middle of the flooded floor with water oozing over onto the carpet, and I screamed in anger--mostly at Gary! I had no clue where the water turn-off was. We had lived in our condominium for over a year, and I had never had any reason to learn where the shut-off valve was. I didn't dare let go of the floater because I knew the water would start flowing again. And it was going to take me time to go into the basement and try to find the turn-off.

I took off my new shoe and propped up the floater (ruined the shoe). The water mostly stopped flowing. By the time I called the condo association and found out where the water turn-off switch was, the bathroom floor, the carpet and padding into both my office and bedroom were soaked through and I had to call the disaster clean-up professionals to come in, pull up the carpet and pad, dry it off with their heating fans, then give it a good cleaning. It cost lots of money

All of a sudden the world fell in on me as I realized that I wasn't dealing with life's issues as well as I thought I was. That was the beginning of my understanding that I *wasn't* going to be all right--that there was a world of things I didn't know, and I *should* know. My ignorance was costing me a lot of time and money, and the stress was overwhelming.

I was becoming increasingly aware of things that were costing me dearly, all because I didn't know any better—things that if only Gary and I had discussed while he was alive, I would not have been as blind-sided as I was. I was also becoming aware that there were many more things I would not have even known to ask him. In other words: I didn't know what I didn't know.

I was in great emotional pain. There just had to be something positive that could come out of this dreadful experience.

INTRODUCTION

PERMISSION GRANTED

or--IF YOU LOVED ME

❮ᴧ❯

Any couple who has been married or together for any length of time knows that the only way the partnership can ever end is either through divorce or death of one of the partners. When recognizing the fact that one or the other of the couple could be single, strange as it may seem, divorce seems to be the easier of the two situations for the partners to seriously discuss. What will it really mean for either of them to be single--again?

When going through a divorce, each party is anxious to get the most residual left-overs possible out of the marriage and, therefore, is eager to determine what the holdings of the marriage are and decide who is going to get what. What and how large are the investments, if any, and what is in the bank accounts? What happens to the life insurance policies and the retirement savings? If the wife brought $20,000 into the marriage, is she going to be able to take it back out of the marriage? Who gets the 4-foot LCD-TV? What is the value of the house and who gets it?

How are the assets to be divided between the two, and will the division be enough to maintain a certain standard of living, or are economic adjustments going to be necessary? Does the wife need to go back to work? Does the husband need to get a second job?

What will happen to the children? Where do they go and how are they to be taken care of---financially and emotionally? What are the arrangements for taking care of them?

When discussing the financial and legal ramifications of a divorce, the husband and wife are usually zealous to do whatever research is necessary to determine what the outcomes for each party will be. The two can usually discuss legal issues: what decisions need to be made and what documents need to be drafted and signed. By the end of the process, each party has a sound awareness of where he or she will stand.

If partners in a marriage are not hesitant to do this type of extensive research when anticipating a divorce, why are they so reluctant to do the same type of examination of their financial circumstances and legal state of affairs when thinking about end-of-life issues?

The answer to that question is easy: because it involves discussing just that---end-of-life issues, which usually makes partners uncomfortable. End-of-life issues "are sticky and morbid and should be reserved for the elderly" (as some say). Unfortunately, unless both partners in the marriage are to die at the same time (probably in an unforeseen accident), one or the other of the couple will be left alone to make a life as a single person. Statistics prove that men die at an earlier age than women do, so in our society it is predominantly the wife who will be the surviving spouse. But not always.

What will this mean? Besides being left alone to cope with *everything*, the most important and imminent factor the surviving spouse is going to deal with is meeting the financial obligations, both monthly responsibilities and those costs that have come because of the death of the spouse. The first issue the surviving spouse is going to be faced with—is there enough money? *Is there enough money?*

13

Not unlike in a divorce, the surviving spouse should have a firm understanding of what the death of a partner will mean financially. The same type of research done when determining the value of the assets during a divorce should be done to determine the value of the assets for a surviving spouse.

My husband passed away in 1999--my, that seems like such a long time ago. Before he died, we had not discussed his death or dying. I did not want to raise uncomfortable issues with him while he was *dying,* for heaven's sake! I made the mistake of thinking that I would be okay after he was gone. I was a professional woman who was pretty savvy about life—finances, taxes, legal issues, etc.—I would be okay.

But I had no idea what was facing me. I was so ill-prepared, and I have paid the price—over and over again. I have paid a financial price, an emotional price, and I have learned.

During this learning process I decided that I could possibly try to save others from the dilemmas I had experienced---all caused by my own ignorance. Because I am a professional instructor, I began giving seminars to groups--the makeup of the groups being exclusively elderly married couples. The main purpose of each seminar was two-fold: (1) to give each couple "permission" to talk to each other about those things that, because they are uncomfortable to discuss, usually remain unsaid; and (2) to give lists of items that should and could be discussed between the two of them—the discussion of which could ultimately serve in helping the remaining spouse to not be as ignorant as I had been after my spouse was gone.

It was while giving these seminars that I became even more profoundly aware of how uneasy the majority of couples are in talking about end-of-life issues and will do almost anything to avoid doing so. They will procrastinate, delay, postpone, defer--whatever it takes to avoid the discussion. No-one wants to admit that even when each of the partners is healthy and viable, that somewhere in a room in the house lurks that shadow of the elephant—the big gray one-- there to remind the couples that one of them will eventually be alone, and that lone person's life is going to go on and will have to be lived. Surprisingly no-one wants to think about what the quality of that life will be, especially if there is a hint that the surviving spouse could be left in an untenable and uncomfortable situation—with no money.

Most often the partners in a healthy marriage know, within their hearts, that this is a discussion that needs to be had! The wife, since she will statistically be the one left behind, really does want to know where she will stand financially. What will be her options? *Will she be okay?*

So what is it that stops couples from having the most important discussion they will ever *need* to have? Is it too hard to look into each other's eyes and have the discussion? Is it that--if you don't talk about it, it won't be there? If you don't talk about the elephant in the room (the impending death of a spouse) then it won't happen?

Or maybe it's just that wonderful word--procrastination--that gets in the way. The parties truly do want to have the discussion. They *mean* to have the discussion. They may have even bantered it about a little bit. But they never seriously seem to get around to it. There never seems to be the incentive that reminds them that it should be done. There never seems to be enough time. Or, perhaps the lack of the discussion is deliberate—that either partner is afraid of how the other will react.

Why should the wife be hesitant to approach the subject with her husband? Will he get angry? Will he be disappointed in her for not trusting his judgment to have taken care of things? Will he be uncomfortable with the subject and decide that he doesn't want to discuss it?

Conversely, for what reasons would a husband not want to discuss these issues with his wife? The husband probably does have a ballpark idea of what his wife's financial situation will be upon his death, but since it involves talking about his death, it could be he doesn't want to broach the subject with her. "What do you want to do—to get rid of me?" he says.

Or perhaps it's the case of the husband wanting to talk about end-of-life issues with his wife, and she refuses: she has been so profoundly dependent on her husband for managing all the business issues of the family, she does not want to talk about it! She pulls back and winces, fluttering her hands at arm's length not wanting to discuss anything! She would prefer to ignore the reality of life (and death), and let happen what will happen.

A few months into giving the seminars, I received a very emotional email from one of my close friends:

15

"I had planned to spend Saturday with my old friend from elementary school. I called Saturday morning to confirm and she told me she had just been told her husband, who was vacationing in Arizona at his sister's home, had died of a massive heart attack. She was in total shock but wanted me to come and be with her. I stayed the better part of the day. I so wished I had heard your lesson on what to do when a spouse dies. All I could remember to tell her was to be sure to get ten death certificates. She said they had not done anything about planning wills or trusts or the like. Is there anything I should tell her? She was absolutely frozen. I feel terrible about her. She was so worried because he had taken care of everything – cars, money, titles, deeds, etc. and she doesn't know where anything is or what to do, so she was feeling regret at not having plowed into that stuff whether he liked it or not – and feeling anger at him because he was so grouchy about her being involved in 'his' business. In addition to that, of course she was crying over her loss. Her daughter and son-in-law and new grandson arrived while I was there and neighbors began to arrive with food so I could see she would be supported and it was okay for me to leave. So here I am now – thinking about how Death follows us everywhere, always, and we should have our houses in order!"

After receiving this email the first thing I did was become very angry! It is so sad and so heart-rending that a surviving spouse has to suffer so. First the spouse suffers over the death of his or her partner, which, believe me, brings interminable pain. Then in addition, the spouse is left with the enormous decisions and choices that need to be made immediately, even while still in the throes of grief--issues that could have been addressed and decisions already made had the couple only had *those* discussions.

There is no reason for a surviving spouse to suffer as this woman did, as I did—and as others have done! I decided right then to make this my mission and my objective—to assist couples through this uncomfortable process, to help them want to talk to each other, to help them make plans, to help them be involved together in this extremely important undertaking so that neither partner, be it the wife nor the husband, is left incapacitated at this time of greatest vulnerability.

I became more and more intent on gathering as much information as I could on what a surviving spouse needs to know. I talked with new widows and widowers. I asked them what was the handful of life's unknown realities that brought immediate anguish and added to the heartache of his or her spouse's death? I read and researched books and news articles.

Each time I gave a seminar I learned something else from the members of my classes. From the questions they asked I learned what items were pertinent, and I added more details to my own lists. More importantly, I came to sympathize with how extremely difficult it is for most couples to discuss these issues. There certainly are those pragmatic souls who can realistically think ahead to death and dying with no uneasiness or qualms, but those are few and far between.

At some point I decided that I needed to write a book—that there was too much information that needed to be gathered, compiled and disseminated for the benefit of other couples who are currently as clueless as I once was.

Fortunately, I am a journal keeper and I have been able to reconstruct old thoughts and, sometimes, painful recollections. I have included some of those remembrances as I have been writing this book. The journal entries are in italics and always include a date. The dates and the snippets of memories will take you through the journey of my husband and me.

It took me a long time to write this book. First of all---I didn't want to. But the more I learned, I realized how many times a simple conversation between the two of us could have saved me so much grief and trouble, as well as a great amount of money, and as I have talked with other widows and widowers, I recognized the need for a book of this kind.

This book can be your incentive. This book can give you the excuse to broach the subject with your spouse. From my experience, one of the partners in the marriage usually feels more comfortable and at ease than the other about discussing these types of issues. I would encourage that gutsy partner to take the initiative and use the ideas in this book as your permission and your incentive to approach these subjects with your partner.

This discussion needs to be had while both partners are vigorous and well and able to make sound decisions. Leaving the discussion to the time when one of the partners is dying is better than doing nothing, but could be extremely painful and not nearly as beneficial.

If, however, you are passed that point where both spouses are healthy and you are now dealing with the impending demise of one of the partners, *it is still not too late.* You now have an even more compelling reason to follow the advice and suggestions in this book, though they may now be more difficult for you to discuss.

More importantly, if you hold these talks while both of you are dynamic and fit (well, ostensibly), your talks will be pragmatic and unthreatening. You can keep your emotions rational and logical and, matter of fact.

You can use this book as your excuse--your reason--to get started. Allow this book to grant you the *PERMISSION* to get started. One or the other of you can take this book to your partner and use it to open the possibly uncomfortable dialogue of end-of-life issues.

Following are a few scenarios to help you open the conversation:

- Did you hear about the Smiths and what a mess they were in when Bob died? Julie had no idea where any of the papers were—whether she had any money or not. We probably ought to be talking about these things right now while we are both healthy, don't you think?

- I really would like to talk about a few things before either one of us gets sick. You know? Just talking about it isn't going to make it happen, and I need to know now, while you are healthy, what you want me to do. What kind of decisions do you want me to make?

- Where is the location of our wills? We do have wills, don't we?

- The doctor said to me the other day that there are some documents I need to sign about end-of-life issues and what I want for medical care. We probably both ought to be involved together in this, don't you think? I would be so grateful just to have an idea about what you are thinking and what you would expect and want me to do if you are unable to tell me.

- If it is, indeed, too overwhelming right now to think about these things, let's make a date sometime in the future when we're both more ready. We can each be thinking about the issues we want to discuss at that time.

If you take the lead and ask the question, and there is no response, wait until there is a better moment. Remind your spouse that you know how difficult this is, but that it is really important for *you* to know what to do when "that" time comes. What does your partner expect of you?

If you are uncomfortable broaching the subject face to face, make a tape recording and suggest that you meet at a certain time. When you are together, begin your conversation by using any one specific chapter in this book as your motivation to do something—anything—to get started.

The book is designed for you to start wherever you feel the most interest. It doesn't need to be read from the beginning to the end. Not every chapter will apply to your personal situation. Begin with the chapter that holds the most relevance for you. Then proceed from there.

To have this conversation is an act of kindness. It is a profound act of loving care on the part of each of you to want your companion to be okay as a surviving spouse.

This book is replete with stories, advice, common sense and many ideas. Please understand that it is *not my intent to give professional advice*. It is important that you remember that I am a mother, a grandmother, a great-grandmother, a professional instructor, a professional writer, and a widow. I am NOT an attorney, a CPA, an investment advisor, a financial planner, a mortician. I was a caregiver, but am not that any more.

I am a layman proposing those discussion issues that I have learned through my own experiences, through other's experiences, and from what I have read and researched. Almost every one of the issues discussed in this book should also be discussed with a professional.

Please use the chapters in this book to discuss with your spouse, to talk with your professional advisors, and to make your own plans based on your own individual status.

Action Items for This Chapter:

(1) As you are reading this, go find your partner. Give him or her a big hug and a kiss and deeply and sincerely profess your love.

(2) Tell your spouse that, in order to demonstrate the deepest aspects of your love, you are embarked on a great adventure, the results of which will make certain that *if* there is a catastrophe and one or the other of you dies, the person who is left to go on alone will be OK. Invite your partner to go on this adventure with you.

(3) Look through this book together, see what it entails, and make a decision as to whether you think it is important for you to gather this information right now or sometime within the next month. Don't put it off longer than that.

(4) Make a commitment to each other that you will do this. In other words, make a promise to each other to do it together!

And remember: To plan for death is not to invite it.

[To the reader: From this point on, the book can be read in any order. Refer first to the chapters that have immediate meaning to you and your needs. Then double back to what you left unread—or leave those chapters totally unread—until the need is there. This book is your resource book to be used as--and when--you need.]

CHAPTER ONE

PRINCE, PAUPER or SCULLERY MAID
--or--CAN I LIVE AS I ALWAYS HAVE?

←∿→

The immediate and most recognizable piece of information you need to have is--what money will be available for maintaining your particular life-style after your spouse is gone? Will you be able to live as you have always lived, or will you need to cut coupons, corners, and cut out driving because of a reduction in income?

Gathering the information listed in this chapter, and doing it together with your significant other, will tell you both exactly what your financial situation is. If you are deeply in debt (or only a little bit in debt) examine the material anyway. Compiling the information is the only way you can face the financial projections that will become very real after the death of either spouse.

Unfortunately, in the baby-boom and older generations (of which I am one) it has been considered, in many cases, the husband's responsibility to do the financial management for the family and not to bother the "little woman" with these issues that are beyond her interest (and probably, she thinks, beyond her capabilities).

Why has this happened--where the wife doesn't have a clue what immediate funds are available, what investment funds there are, what the pension realities are, and anything else having to do with finances?

Though certainly not universal, sometimes the husband feels as though that's his purview---that he doesn't interject himself into his wife's responsibilities in the home and he doesn't want her interjecting herself into his realm. There can be many reasons for this attitude: sometimes it's a power play in the family where the husband wants to have that financial control over his wife and the family--and that can be pretty intimidating.

Most commonly, however, the older wife really does not want to be bothered with such a consuming part of the family responsibility and accountability. Her attitude is, she's been relying on her husband to handle the finances and it's been working fine for as long as they have been married—why should she be bothered with it? She is content to handle her part of the budget that allows for paying for the groceries and a few sundry household items. Carried to the far extreme, the wife has not even paid any of the monthly bills.[1]

There are obviously many variations of the above extremes. But, for the most part in the older generations, the major portion of financial management has been left to the husband.

Fortunately in the newer and younger generations (Gen X, Gen Y, Millennials—are there any more?) the husband and wife have had a better melding of family responsibilities. The husband is typically more involved in the daily activities of raising the children and in the responsibilities of helping in the home, and the wife usually has a job of her own where she brings in part of the family income. As a result, the wife is generally more involved in what is happening with family finances.

The unfortunate reality, however, is that no matter what the situation is in the family, the majority of spouses still do not discuss the probability of being left alone to deal with all the money issues if one or the other of the partners dies. And more particularly, if the couple is still young with young children, their sense of

---

[1] Ellen Hoffman, "When Couples Clam Up" AARP Bulletin June 2002

invulnerability is strong--they don't think it's possible that anything could happen to one or the other of them. Wrong!!

I tell the following personal story to highlight the unreliability of what money you might think you have, and to point out that, as the surviving spouse, you need to be resourceful and looking at all options of any possible income.

In mine and Gary's case, I was the partner who had done most of the money management. There actually had been not much to manage: salaries we each brought to the table, a couple of IRA accounts, some CDs and a couple of life insurance policies. The previous year, Gary and his partner had sold their business on a contract to a former employee. The monthly payment was to provide a retirement stream-of-income to us. I was gravely concerned about the contract issue, but decided I should stay out of it.

Gary and I also owned a couple of duplexes that were free and clear. The rental income would certainly help. We also owned a cabin—free and clear. But there was a lot of pricey maintenance and expenditures on both of the properties.

After Gary's death I learned of a death benefit from the musicians union that Gary and I had both belonged to in our younger years. I was given the option of taking the lump sum death benefit of $2000 or of taking a monthly payment *for the rest of my life* of $83. I was 61 years old at the time, and it did not take too much figuring to determine that if I lived only 25 more months (at $83/month), I would outlive the worth of $2000. Taking only $83 a month doesn't sound like much but it would clearly bring me the greater overall lifetime benefit.

With the income from the contract, the rentals and my salary, I had determined that I would have approximately the same monthly income after Gary's death as I currently had. Until I retired, my lifestyle would not change significantly--I thought.

Within a year after Gary's death my financial plans went berserk. First, the man who had purchased Gary's business defaulted on the contract. And, worse yet, Gary's partner and I were sued because the new owner had not paid a sizable invoice, and the company who was owed the money went after the two of us, not realizing (or so they said) that the business had been sold to someone else.

The new owner testified in court that he had no money. Taking pity on the vendor who did not get paid, the judge, in his wisdom, ordered that we (Gary's partner and I) should pay the invoice. So coughing up that amount of money, plus the attorney's fees, took a mighty bite.

> *Jan 25/2001 – My second birthday without Gary. Things are going pretty much okay, but money is certainly tight. Mo [Gary's partner] has ended up selling off most of the large equipment but I think I've still got to be in a better situation than they are. At least I have my state retirement. I'm thinking of answering a couple of RFPs [Requests for Proposal] to see if maybe I can pick up a couple of contract writing jobs. If I could get one or two of those a year, it would certainly help.*

I was retired by now and obviously needed to find other sources of income to maintain any barely acceptable style of living, minimal as it was. From Gary's two life insurance policies I had immediate money that would help to alleviate some of the problems. I was anxious, however, not to deplete those funds entirely because I knew that I would need some long-term financial stability.

I received what, for me, was some sound financial advice *for my particular situation.* I was introduced to the "annuity." My annuities have all matured at this writing, and I now have a monthly income from those for the rest of my life. Annuities are discussed in more detail later in this chapter.

The other immediate income possibility was to go back to work-- not to an outside office, but to stay at home and do what contract writing I could to earn a few extra dollars. Fortunately a few people still remembered me and were willing to hire me for some contract work.

I was fortunate to have a variety of income possibilities. As you and your partner are determining what income either of you will have as a surviving spouse, don't overlook the many possible resources that might be out there.

INCOME AND OUTGO (Here it comes--There it goes)

Of primary importance to you and your loved ones is the most basic question: *How much monthly income will there be for the surviving spouse in order to pay the monthly living expenses?* It could not be more simple than that.

24

Will you be able to maintain your current standard of living? Will you be able to stay in your current home, or will there be a need to move to a smaller home or apartment? Will you have enough money to cover your medical costs? Will you be struggling to make ends meet?

Or, conversely, will there now be more money than you have ever had? Will you be able to travel or to spoil yourself? Will you be able to do those things you have always wanted to do but never could because there was not enough money? Or time? Or, freedom? These figures should be easy to pull together, and what a surprise (and a blessing) that would be if you were to discover something you hadn't thought of. Knowing your income is important, but you also need to know what your monthly expenses are. Those figures are easier to obtain since you deal with them on a monthly basis. But we'll look at that later.

NET MONTHLY INCOME – POSSIBLE SOURCES

To determine your NET MONTHLY INCOME, tally all possible sources of monthly income and then deduct your federal and state *monthly* income taxes. This gives you your approximate Net Monthly Income. Do this same exercise for each partner, because each conclusion will be different. Using the following items as prompts, look for every possible income resource you can think of. Remember--analyze the income for each partner. Even if one of the partners has no current income, that's important information to work from.

As you are gathering this financial information, at the same time—and in a separate notebook (or computer file)—compile all the data concerning each individual account; e.g., names, account numbers, balances, etc. Refer to the APPENDIX for the specific information you need to obtain on each item (insurance, stocks, bonds, savings accounts, etc.).

With all of this detailed material now in one place, recognize that this information is extremely valuable and should be safely kept where no-one else can have access to it. For hard copies, store in a safe deposit box. If compiled on a computer, save the file on a flash drive, delete the information from the computer, and store the flash drive in a safe deposit box. Make certain your attorney and/or your partner has knowledge of where this information is being kept.

Salary: If the deceased spouse was working, that salary will no longer be available. But if you (be you widow or widower) are working, list your net income--the income from your salary after taxes. This figure is whatever your monthly check(s) says--in other words, your take-home pay.

Pension/Retirement Funds: This figure can be a little tricky because, as a couple you might already be living on your spouse's retirement pension. But once your spouse dies, will you still be entitled to that pension? Does your pension have survivor benefits? In most cases, in order for the married employee to exclude spousal benefits, pension plans require a signed release from that excluded spouse. You both need to check with the employer who is paying the pension (or will be paying the pension) and determine whether the remaining spouse is entitled to keep receiving those same monies. Sometimes the answer is--no. Or sometimes the answer is yes, but the amount will be reduced by a certain percentage. This is a critical piece of information you need to have.

Social Security: Most Americans have paid into Social Security and we expect it to be there with a monthly stipend if and when we qualify for it. Currently, that is the plan; however there may be some restructuring of Social Security in the future. There are many different constraints that determine what each individual person is entitled to. This depends on contributions into the system over the person's working life, and depending on what age you choose to begin withdrawing benefits. Effective Social Security planning needs to take place well in advance of planned retirement, as benefits while living and survivor benefits will be impacted. A visit to the local Social Security office is imperative so you can consult with a qualified advisor.

A widow can collect benefits on the death of her husband, and if she can live on those lower widow benefits and wait until the age of 70 to withdraw the money from her own Social Security account, the benefits she will receive on her own account may significantly increase. Even if the woman has been divorced from the ex-husband who dies, there may be a benefit due to her. For general information you can access the Social Security web site at www.ssa.gov.

There is no way of knowing what your personal benefits will be without visiting the Social Security office. Call first and make an appointment, or take a good book to read. You will be in line for a long time.

Investments: Hopefully you have paid for many years into a retirement account such as a traditional IRA or Roth plan, or some sort of tax-deferred retirement plan. If you are fortunate, your employer will have been adding matching funds. Some plans mandate that you start withdrawing from those accounts at age 70. Will you be drawing down those accounts monthly, quarterly or annually? Also, many have "dabbled" in the stocks and bonds markets. This may be the time to set up a secure monthly income from these investments. Talk to the stock brokers or financial advisors who are handling your accounts and get their advice on what should be done with your money. These professionals make money only when they can sell you something. There is absolutely nothing wrong with this provided you are knowledgeable about the purchases you are making and have an understanding of what they mean to your own portfolio.

Annuities: An annuity is a guaranteed sum paid to you for life from a life insurance company. You can purchase an annuity with the money from an insurance death benefit, a pension distribution, possible money from an inheritance, or the like. The funds can accumulate tax-deferred until maturity, at which time the benefit can be paid in a variety of ways; i.e., a lump- sum payout, monthly installments, or some other combinations of pay-out. With some strategies, even if the annuity-holder outlives the balance of the annuity, the monthly benefits will still be paid. Obviously, the financial strength of the insurance company is important. Speak to a life insurance agent or your financial advisor for definitive information as to what would work for you.

Rental income: If you are fortunate enough (or unfortunate enough) to own rental properties, you have income from the monthly rent payments. There will, of course, be expenditures, but don't consider those right now. They will be covered later.

27

Reverse Mortgage: In a reverse mortgage, the homeowner can use the equity in his/her home to live on. The money is paid from the bank to the homeowner however the homeowner dictates: cash, monthly payments, line-of-credit--whatever the homeowner wants or needs. The best part is there are no payments due back to the lender until the homeowner moves, sells the property, or dies. Consider this only if you don't intend to bequeath the equity in your home to your kids. What a dilemma---your well-being, or your kid's well-being? Check with a licensed mortgage broker for information on how to obtain a reverse mortgage.[2]

Accounts Receivable: If you or your spouse have sold something to someone (an automobile, a house, jewelry, etc.) and that person is making monthly payments to you on the item, include that amount. Do you know where the paperwork is that confirms this sale? Don't overlook the loans made to a child (or, children).

Miscellaneous Additional Funds: There may be other instances in which there could be other reliable, monthly incomes. Something as simple as a monthly withdrawal from a savings account could qualify.

Once you have identified all the possible monthly income you can receive from as many sources as possible, tally it all up. If you haven't already done so, next deduct your federal and monthly taxes, and the balance will be your probable Net Monthly Income. Hopefully you will be delighted with the figure you see, and you can now rest secure in knowing there will be enough income for the remaining spouse to comfortably live.

MONTHLY OUTGO

But, not so fast--before you can be assured your monthly income is going to be enough, you need to have a sound understanding of how much money you are spending each month. Create a tally of all of your "outgo"—that which you are consistently spending on a monthly basis. Many of these expenses you will need to tally on an annual basis then divide by twelve for an average monthly figure. Watch out for those out-of-pocket expenditures.

---

[2] Jane Bryant Quinn, "Financially Speaking" AARP Bulletin March 2012

Mortgage/rent payments: What are your expenditures to keep a roof over your head? This number includes only the monthly cost for you to live where you do (utilities are a line item of their own to be accounted for later).

Food: The next largest expenditure in most people's budget is food. It's critical that you understand how much money you spend in addition to your groceries—eating out, fast food, coffee kiosks, vending machine snacks---the dimes and quarters you spend without thinking too much about it. Keep track of those.

Transportation: How do you travel from one place to the next— your own automobile? Motorcycle? Public transportation? Taxi? If you own and drive a car, include the expenses of running the car— gas, registration, maintenance, tires, taxes, insurance. You get the picture.

Clothing: What do you spend for your clothes? You may need to figure this on an annual basis then divide by twelve in order to calculate an average monthly figure. Do you make your own clothes? Include in this category the sewing costs for fabric, patterns, threads, buttons, zippers, etc.

Utilities: These figures are the easiest to obtain because you can readily dig out all your paid monthly utility bills. The bills will probably fluctuate with the weather and the seasons, so determine an annual total then divide by twelve for a monthly average.

Housing Costs: What are your average costs for maintaining your home? What do you spend on repairs, insurance, property taxes, furniture, yard equipment, appliances, etc.?

Work Expenses: Do you work from home? Does your job require you to pay for certain items such as travel, office supplies, business cards, equipment, or such?

Education: Are you paying on old student loans? Are you paying for something other than public education for your children? Are there additional expenses for your children such as sports, cheerleading, field trips, etc.? Are you a reader who spends money on books? Are you taking any courses--online or otherwise?

Entertainment: Do you attend plays, movies, concerts? Or do you go to the park and throw a Frisbee with your dog? Entertainment can mean different things to different people. But if you are spending money on what you do, tally it in this line item.

Medical: These costs can be tricky depending on whether you are paying in total for your (and your family's) health costs, or whether medical insurance is paid by your employer. What are you paying out-of-pocket on an annual basis for your medical costs? Don't forget your co-pays.

Donations: Except for church tithes and offerings, for the most part these are expenses that are not paid on a monthly basis. If you are in the habit of giving a dollar here and there to the panhandlers, that can add up.

Hobbies: Most of us have our own little passions to spend time and money on—some quite costly, and others, not so costly.

Miscellaneous: You and your spouse are the only two people who can complete this category, because we all spend our own money in our own way. Slipping a buck (or more) to a grandchild now and then may not seem important enough to tally. But when you don't keep track of the incidentals, it's easy to go astray. Any time you pay cash for something, here's where you can lose control of your expenditures.

Hopefully, now you can subtract these figures from the Monthly Income figures. If you can't, you can at least understand whether the surviving spouse is going to be okay, or whether he or she is going to need to make adjustments of some kind.

LUMP SUM BENEFITS PAID UPON YOUR SPOUSE'S DEATH

Of no small consequence will be income derived from the death benefits that will be paid after the death of a spouse. Here again, make an accounting of death benefits for each partner as they will surely be different for each. Some of the following can be possible sources of death benefits:

Life Insurance: Hopefully you have one or two--or more--policies of life insurance. It doesn't matter what type of policy it is (see CHAPTER TWO for an explanation of the types of insurance policies), it will have a death benefit and you should know how much that is. Don't be confused with the Cash Value. There is a difference between that and the death benefit(s). Check with your life insurance agent.

Social Security: As of this writing there is a death benefit from Social Security. It's only a pittance and may not seem worth going after--but trust me. When the funeral costs start to hit you, you will be glad for any amount. You will need to apply for it at your local Social Security office.

Union: If your spouse belonged to a union, sometimes there will be a death benefit. Even if your spouse has not been a union member for many years, check that possibility.

Veterans Benefits: If your spouse was a veteran, there is available a reimbursement of some burial and burial plot expenses. Depending on the circumstances of the death, the veteran's discharge status, and whether there is financial need will determine the amount of assistance available. Contact the Veterans Administration in your state for complete information.

From work: Make certain there is no unpaid salary that is owing. Sometimes it is a shot in the dark, but there might be accumulated vacation or sick leave that has some monetary value. Also check to see if there is a death benefit that is connected to your spouse's pension. There may also be a group term life insurance death benefit.

Workman's Compensation Fund: If the death is work related, there may be benefit funds available. Contact the department in your state that regulates the Workman's Compensation Fund.

Creditor Insurance: Some credit cards carry insurance that will pay off the balance of the credit card upon the death of the card holder. You may need to research this with the credit card company. There may be similar benefits through your credit union.

THE REST OF THE STORY – YOUR NET WORTH

After you have established what your monthly income and outgo requirements are for you to live on a daily basis, you still need to do more research to uncover the rest of your financial situation. If your income is less than what you are paying out, don't fret--you are in good company, and your financial picture may not be as bleak as it seems depending on other assets that you might have.

You need to know if you owe more money than the assets you have (over and above what your monthly income is). What this dollar amount is will determine your Net Worth---your assets minus your liabilities. Learning what your net worth is will help you know whether you are living in the "red" or in the "black." Knowing your overall financial situation can either give you a sense of financial security, or it can give you the information you need for planning how to get out of debt.

Having immediate access to your assets upon the death of your spouse will depend on how the assets are held and in whose name they are held. If both of your names are on the accounts (savings, money markets, CDs, etc.) the surviving spouse can immediately access the accounts. Title to your real estate will transfer to the surviving spouse if the property is held as joint tenants or tenancy by the entirety, whichever is recognized in your state. And it will save you hassle and trouble if both of your names are on the title to the car(s). The car is much easier to sell.

Putting all of your assets in both names, however, might pose a problem if the combined value of your assets is high enough to be taxed for estate taxes. This is the time when you need an estate planning attorney to help you through this maze.

What happens if some of your accounts and/or other assets are in only your name or your spouse's name and either of you dies? Much depends on what state you are living in and what the inheritance laws are. In the majority of instances, the assets will need to go through probate and a judge will decided where they will go. This is when it is imperative that you have a will and/or a living trust (see CHAPTER TWO).

In verifying what your assets are, look at *everything* you own that could be potentially sold or cashed in, and what amount of money would be generated if you were to do so. *This does not mean that you are expected to sell off your assets!* This exercise will just give you a clearer snapshot of your value (what you are worth).

ASSETS

Here again, as you are gathering this financial information, at the same time—and in a separate notebook (or computer file)—compile all the data concerning each individual account. Refer to the APPENDIX for the specific information you need to obtain on each item (insurance, stocks, bonds, savings accounts, etc.).

Cash: What amount of immediate cash do you have on hand such as a large roll of cash in your pocket, or do you have cash stowed away somewhere (hopefully someplace really safe, and not in a mattress).

Bank Accounts: If both of your names are on the accounts (a savings account, a checking account and/or a money market account) the funds can be immediately and fully withdrawn by the surviving party with no penalties or complications.

Certificates of Deposit: CDs are a very safe investment in that you know exactly what your return will be. You can invest in a CD at any bank or credit union. You will be committed to leaving your money in the CD for a predetermined length of time, and if you withdraw your money early, you will pay a penalty. As with bank accounts and after the death of your spouse, easy and quick access will depend on whose name is on the CD.

Real Estate: What is the appraised value of any real estate you own; e.g., your home, rentals, second homes (cabins, condos), vacant land, commercial real estate owned by you, or any other type of real property? In the most recent financial collapse of the real estate market, the value of your holdings may have been reduced dramatically so it is important that you have a realistic assessment made of what you own. The good news is that the market is recovering. As a result, the most accurate assessment really can only be made by a licensed real estate appraiser.

For these purposes right now, consider only the current value of the property and do not take into account what your real estate equities are, which is the value of your property minus the balance owed on your mortgage (if any). That amount will be taken into account later in the chapter.

Pension Fund: What is your current vesting status? Do you need to work more years to be fully vested? Do you have the option of taking a lump sum or an annuity? What would that amount be?

Mutual Fund: A mutual fund is created when many people pool their money and invest in a common, diversified group of securities. If you are part of a mutual fund you will own a proportionate share of the mutual fund. How much is your share and what is its value?

Stocks and Bonds: If you were to sell your stocks or bonds, what amount of money would that generate? As the stock market fluctuates, you might have to determine a monthly average of the current market value of what you own.

U.S. Government Bonds: U.S. treasury securities are considered to be the safest of all investments. These include EE and HH bonds and other treasury bills and notes. Treasury securities have either a fluctuating rate of interest or a fixed rate of interest, so if you are holding these types of bonds or notes you need to check with your personal bank or credit union to determine what the market values of these holdings are.

Tax Deferred Accounts: The best known of these accounts is an IRA (Individual Retirement Account). Also included are 401(k) and 403(b) plans, and Keogh plans. These are retirement plans to which individuals can contribute pre-tax funds. Taxes are paid when the funds are withdrawn, assuming that you will be in a lower tax bracket at that time. These funds can either be guaranteed fixed accounts or variable accounts that have been invested in a variety of stocks and bonds. In some instances, your employer may also contribute to your account. You will need to do the research to determine the current value of these accounts.

Life Insurance (cash value): Your life insurance policy may have a cash value that you can borrow against. This is another asset to use in helping determine your net worth.

Annuities: After you have invested with an insurance company, and upon maturation of your annuity contract, you are paid either a lump sum, monthly payments or some other pay-out combination to which you agree. List the total amount of the Ending Contract Value.

Inheritances: Usually, the possibility of receiving an inheritance (money, art, jewelry, personal effects, etc.) is too tenuous to be counted as a declared asset. However, if you are very certain that Aunt Polly has bequeathed her $10,000 diamond ring to you in her will, you could probably be assured of counting that as an asset (barring anything unforeseen happening).

Cars, RVs, Boats,: In order to determine what these items are worth, use the Blue Book values of each.

Accounts Receivable: If individuals are paying you back for money you have loaned them or are paying you for an item you have sold to them, the balance of the money that is owed to you is an account receivable. Do not list the monthly payment that is sent to you---list the total amount that is owed to you. If you have already listed the amount due to you on a real estate contract, do not include that again on this section.

Precious Metals: Gold is currently a popular and valued commodity. As of this writing, gold prices are very high and, as a result, many people are selling their gold jewelry pieces. Most other metals do not have the same values that gold does.

Collectibles/Art/Jewelry/etc.: A collection of specific items can be extremely valuable to the owner who has done the collecting over many years, but can be of no value to another person. For that reason it is important to have an appraised value made of your

35

collectibles. Value is determined by what someone else would be willing to pay for your specific item(s). A distinction should be made between an appraised value and an insurance value. An insurance value would be the amount of money that the item(s) should be insured for if it would be necessary to replace the item(s). The insurance value usually will be higher than the appraised value. In determining the value of the item as an asset, you would be safest to use the appraised value.

Personal Property/Clothing/Household/Furnishings/ Antiques: There can be significant value in your household furnishings, especially if you were to take into consideration an expensive bedroom or living room set. Some items of clothing (leather or furs) may retain their worth. Antiques (that are not considered to be collectibles) will maintain their value, but other furnishings (and clothing) can depreciate. In determining what estimation to apply to them consider the depreciated value--what amount could you sell the item for in its current condition?

While you are collecting this information and calculating the value of your assets, this is the perfect time for you to make a detailed description of your valuables (your collectibles, jewelry, furniture, etc.) and even make a pictorial record of those assets. Open your drawers and look in all your closets. You may discover items you had forgotten.

Making this type of a digital or video record is a valuable thing to do for many reasons. First of all it helps you to assess and document the cash value of each item you have. Also, it is a valuable record to have in case you need to document your losses for an insurance claim (such as in a fire claim).

LIABILITIES (WHAT DO I OWE AND TO WHOM?)

You have now discovered how wealthy you are with everything that you own. Unfortunately, you now have to subtract the debts (liabilities) you have. What do you owe to someone/anyone else? Liabilities are considered to be those obligations that are being paid off usually in prorated amounts, mostly, but not always, on a monthly basis.

You will need to get some legal advice on this, but it might be that some of the liabilities won't impact the gross estate. In other words, if some assets are not held jointly and the obligations of some of the debts are not joint obligations, some debts may be discharged at the death of the debtor. Check with your estate attorney if you have questions on this.

For obligations that will take longer than twelve months to pay off, indicate the *entire balance* of the loan. For monthly obligations such as lease payments, child support, etc., multiply those monthly payments by twelve in order to get an annualized amount. In other words, how much money do you spend for those monthly obligations each year?

Real Estate Mortgage (home): A real estate mortgage is usually the greatest financial obligation a married couple will have. The monthly payments are important for determining your monthly output, but for determining your financial liability, list the entire balance of your loan. Discuss, between the two of you, the type of mortgage you have (interest only? amortized? ARM?). Have an understanding of the breakdown of the monthly payments as to how much goes towards the principal, interest, taxes, insurance and/or a mortgage insurance premium (if any).

Other Real Estate Mortgages (investments, second homes, etc.): If you are fortunate enough to be able to have invested in other forms of real estate, list the balance(s) of any of those mortgage or trust deed loans.

Bank or Credit Union Loans: Indicate the entire balance(s) of loans that are signature loans or lines-of-credit (that don't require you to use your home as a security).

Automobile loans(s): What balance do you owe on your car loan(s), if any?

Credit Card(s): Unfortunately the "loan" granted to you each time you use your credit card is too easy to obtain—all you have to do is use your credit card. But not paying off your credit card obligation in full, especially if you are adding to the balance each month, gets to be an insidious debt and the balance can be a significant liability. Paying the monthly minimum amount required only gets you in deeper.

Education (student loans): These are loans that you are either paying off for your own education or for your children's education. List the entire balance.

Home Improvement Loans: Any remodeling improvements you have made on your home (or any rentals you may own), including painting and/or carpeting, are considered a liability. Include also purchases--on account--of furniture, appliances, etc. Here again, list the entire balances.

Current Recurring Debts: These would be expenses that occur every year, such as property taxes and insurance payments. If you pay on an apartment lease, annualize that amount (multiply by 12). Calculate what you pay annually for all of your utilities. If you pay alimony and/or child support, include that annual amount.

Other Installment Debts: If there are any other debts you are paying, include them on this line (annualized).

(SAMPLE FORM TO USE)

ASSETS	LIABILITIES
Cash_____	Real Estate Mortgage (home)____
Bank Accounts _____	Other Real Estate Mortgages
Certificates of Deposit_____	(investments, second homes,
Real Estate _____	etc_____
Mortgage Insurance_____	Bank or Credit Union Loans____
Pension Fund_____	Automobile Loans(s)_____
Mutual Fund_____	Credit Card(s)_____
Stocks and Bonds_____	Education (student loans)_____
U.S. Government Bonds _____	Home Improvement Loans_____
Tax Deferred Accounts_____	Current Recurring Debts_____
Life Insurance cash value)_____	Other Installment Debts_____
Annuities_____	
Inheritances_____	TOTAL _____
Cars, RVs, Boats_____	
Accounts Receivable_____	
Precious Metals_____	
Collectibles/art/jewelry/etc.___	
Personal Property/Clothing____	
Household	
Furnishings/Antiques_____	
TOTAL _____	

NET WORTH TABULATION

TOTAL ASSETS $_____

MINUS TOTAL LIABILITIES --$_____

NET WORTH =$_____

Whew! That was one heck of a lot of work!! And why should you pull out all those facts and figures? Following are the three best reasons for doing all that research and gathering all that information:

(1) The greatest benefit is that you will not be blind-sided upon the death of your spouse. If you are the surviving partner, you will know exactly what your financial status is now and what it will be on the death of your spouse.

(2) You are now aware of the needs to make adjustments in your net worth while there is still time. Provided you find it necessary, you might need to get an additional job, put away more money into your tax deferred accounts (hopefully you have one or two), or do whatever is necessary to get yourself in a better financial situation.

(3) The partner who has not been included in the financial decisions is at a serious disadvantage and could be gravely incapacitated upon the death of his or her spouse. If only one of the couple has previously been handling all the financial matters, each partner will now be aware of what the financial capacity is of the family.

Gathering this information is going to be a time-consuming and, perhaps, a painful task. You may look on it as being tedious and of having no value. If you are not in the best financial condition with many debts, you may especially be embarrassed to admit what the numbers are telling you. This is exactly the time for you to face the facts---for yourself and for your partner.

Don't allow your spouse to be caught off-guard at your passing. Even if you are in debt, he or she will at least be aware of the situation and can be better prepared, *especially if your spouse will be inheriting some of those debts.*

Financial understanding needs to be honest and straight forward, and each spouse needs to be actively involved, whether he or she wants to, or not, or whether the spouse controlling the finances wants to, or not.

No longer should the partner doing the financial planning not be inclusive of the other partner.

But more than all that, after completing this study you will have reached the original goal that is the focus of this chapter--assuring that the surviving spouse will be left in a comfortable financial position.

Action Items for This Chapter:

(1) Gather together as much of your financial information, at the same time, as you can. You will discover that a great portion of it is in the same place, which will make the task significantly easier.

(2) While all the documents are in front of you, in a separate file or folder make an accounting of each individual item (savings accounts, insurance policies, etc.)

- Use the information found in the APPENDIX to help you identify what you should have for each financial item, such as account numbers, location of documents, balances, etc.

(3) Once the above documentation has been compiled all in one place, and recognizing that this is invaluable information, store the records securely, such as in a safe deposit box. You do not want to allow this information to fall into the wrong hands.

CHAPTER TWO

INSURANCE, TRUSTS and WILLS, OH MY
--or--PUTTING IT BLUNTLY, WHO GETS WHAT?

‹∿›

Other facets for preparing for and/or assisting a spouse to be alone are those of Insurance Planning and Estate Planning. Most people understand if you have a life insurance policy that, on your death, there will be money that goes to the persons you have indicated should receive it. That is a distinct benefit to a surviving spouse.

What most people don't understand or provide for is planning for the distribution of personal assets. Thinking ahead and doing some paperwork can save untold amounts of grief for the survivor.

But let's first talk about Insurance.

INSURANCE PLANNING

What is life insurance? Life insurance is for the purpose of replacing income. Life insurance is the gift that each partner can give to the other. It is the gift of sustenance that replaces your lost income.

If you have a life insurance policy, you have a contract with a life insurance company agreeing that if you make timely premium payments and, if you die, the insurance company will pay a specific amount of money to your beneficiaries. The insurance money you receive is non-taxable--you don't need to pay income tax on the proceeds. Once the money is disbursed, it can be used for anything-- medical bills, college education, funeral costs, a European cruise. There are no limitations on how the money can be spent.

There are several varieties of life insurance from which to choose, and because policies vary from company to company it would be wise to consult with either an insurance agent or a financial planner for specific information on the various policies. The three most popular policies are Term Life Insurance, Whole Life Insurance and Universal Life Insurance---the latter two are often referred to as "permanent" or "cash value" life insurance.

When learning about the policies, there may be several questions to ask about each policy: can you cash in the policy? Can you borrow against the policy? Can you convert the policy to paid-up insurance or to extended-term insurance?

Remember that even though an insurance policy appears to have expired, it may still have some cash value.

TERM LIFE INSURANCE

Term Life Insurance is a policy that provides coverage for a specific period of time such as one year, five years, ten years, etc., but does need to be renewed periodically (usually annually). When you no longer pay your premiums, you will no longer have life insurance.

Term insurance is usually less expensive than cash value life insurance. The younger you are when you purchase the insurance, the lower will be the premium. As you age, term insurance becomes more difficult to obtain, and when you reach 75--85, most term policies stop covering you.

Term insurance is usually taken to cover the breadwinner--the spouse bringing the most money into the family. There can be fairly substantial coverage costing less money than the other policies and, in some cases, can be used to create a comfortable estate for those who are left behind.

WHOLE LIFE INSURANCE

Whole Life Insurance is permanent insurance for as long as you live and continue to make the premium payments. Some of the money that you pay accumulates into a guaranteed cash value, and if you choose to surrender the policy at some time in the future, the cash value will be returned to you.

One of the benefits of a Whole Life policy is that you can borrow against the cash value usually at a lower interest rate than the banks would charge. If you were to die, however, before the loan is paid in full, the amount owing would be reduced from the death benefit.

Remember that the benefits received are income tax free and are usually used to cover expenses, such as medical expenses, taxes and/or other debts. Or, one can choose to go to school or go on a trip—the money is there to spend as the beneficiary would wish.

Even if you have allowed the policy to expire, there may still be some cash value benefit.

UNIVERSAL LIFE INSURANCE

Universal Life Insurance provides many of the advantages of a whole life policy such as protection for as long as you live and the accumulation of a cash value. There is greater flexibility for coverage amounts and premium payments. And the dividends are calculated differently because of the investment in the stock market.

BENEFICIARIES

Life insurance policies are not specifically part of your estate planning other than to know what the payout of the policy is for the remaining beneficiaries. A beneficiary is the person who "benefits" from the policy. Life insurance benefits do not have to go through probate (see that section later in this chapter), but are paid out to whomever the policy indicates. It is important that you keep your beneficiary list updated, or your money might not go where you want (e.g., to your first wife whose name is still on the policy).

It should be noted that many life insurance companies have recently added a no-cost critical illness rider to their cash value policies. This allows pre-death access to portions of the death benefit to use for long-term care related needs.

ESTATE PLANNING

Most adults in the United States do not have a will. One can only wonder over the variety of reasons and excuses for not doing so:

- "Estate planning is for the wealthy. I have hardly anything to leave, so there's no reason for me to make a will."
- "My wife/husband gets everything. She/he will take care of it."
- "If I make a will then I will die."
- "Everyone knows what I want to have done with my things---I'll just leave it up to my family."
- "Even if I make a will, everything has to go through probate anyway."
- "I know it's important. I'll get around to doing it really soon."
- "I'm not quite ready. I need to see how my kids treat me before I decide who's going to get what."
- "It's too costly."[3]

An answer to all of the above statements is: no, no and no. The above reasons (and many more) indicate a serious misunderstanding of the needs for estate planning. Most often estate planning is looked upon as being expensive, unnecessary, and a waste of time and money. Hopefully, after reading this chapter, you will see the value of creating a will and/or a living trust, and what the hazards are of failing to do so.

Deciding now what you want to have done after your death with your money, investments, properties, physical holdings, etc., is a way of protecting and providing for your loved ones. And just how you go about doing that will make the difference between grief and agony--or support and security--for those you leave behind. And that will all be determined based on the vehicle you choose to disburse your assets.

At this point I need to reiterate that I am not an attorney. The following information is for your use, to educate you and give you a working knowledge of the items you will want to discuss with your spouse and with your attorney while doing your own estate planning. The Internet will provide many versions of the forms being discussed in this chapter, and therein lies the

---

[3] Sandra Block, "Managing Your Money" <u>USA Today</u> 23 Oct. 2009 p 38

danger. You need to use the version of the form that is valid in your state and that is applicable to the type of assets you hold. This is not a do-it-yourself project. If you want to, however, you might get some forms off the web and start filling them in. But please make certain that an attorney gives the final okay as to their accuracy and validity.

It would be unnatural for you not to want everything that you have attained in this life to go to those people you love the most and who you feel are the most deserving of what you are leaving. The worst thing that could happen--for you and your loved ones--would be for your assets to be diluted through taxes and legal costs or, worse yet, for your wishes to be ignored and for others--not of your choosing--to benefit from your holdings. More than once one hears the horror stories of second spouses--and children--inheriting what should have gone to the children from the original marriage. (Think of the "Cinderella" story.)

Now is the time for you to become your own, best advocate. Now is the time for you to make your wishes known. It is a mistake for you to think that you don't have enough, let alone own enough, to bother with. You have accumulated a lifetime of possessions. You probably have life insurance, savings, pension benefits. And what about that LCD-TV, your favorite chair, all your tools, your father's gold ring that you inherited? What about any of those very special items in your life, expensive or not that you treasure? Do you want them to be cavalierly dealt with and given away (or sold on EBay) with no thought?

More importantly—what about your underage children? If something disastrous were to happen to both you and your spouse, where should your children go and who should care for them? Have you appointed guardians for your children, and have those persons agreed--*in writing*--to take on this responsibility? Whom could you trust to financially manage your assets on your children's behalf until they come of age? And when your children do reach their majority (come of age), would they be ready to manage a large inheritance? Or would you want to still control their legacy for a few more years by confirming that your money would go for specific purposes, such as their buying a house or completing their education? These are issues you don't want to leave to someone else to decide! You especially don't want to leave it for the courts to make the decisions!

It is relatively simple for you to maintain that control, even after your death, provided that is your wish.

In addition, there are other end-of-life issues regarding your health and well-being that you want to decide for yourself while you are still competent and of sound mind (while you still know what you are doing and thinking): what kind of medical treatment do you want to have when you are no longer able to speak for yourself? What level of care do you want to have, and where do you want to live your last days? Who do you want to be your spokesperson at this time, and is it someone you can trust implicitly? These issues will be covered in detail in CHAPTER FIVE on CAREGIVING, but they still have relevance to the issues in this chapter.

WHY DO I NEED A WILL?

For one minute--envision that you have passed away and you have left no will or directive to your family and friends that would indicate what should be done with all of your tangible holdings--your furniture, your TV, your books, your jewelry, your wall hangings-- anything that you have enjoyed while living in your home. Your spouse assumes everything will go to him or her---but maybe not.

Envision friends and relatives descending on your home laying claim to many items in your house. Think about Grandma's ring that she specifically gave to you and put on your finger, and you, in turn, had always promised it to your daughter. Now, after your death, your cousin claims it belongs to her. And imagine two of your sons arguing over something of yours that both of them want to have-- both swearing that you gave it to them. This could be easily taken care of if you had a will. A will is a legal written document that designates how and to whom you want your assets distributed at your death.

INTESTATE

If you die Intestate (without a will), the laws of the state that you have declared as your principal residence at the time of your death (where you pay your state taxes) will, on your behalf in probate court,

47

decide where your assets are to go.[4] Usually the courts will distribute your estate to your spouse and children according to the probate laws of that state, but that might not necessarily be the best thing--or what you want. It can get very confusing if there are previous spouses and children from other marriages.

There may be guardianships of minor children, or elderly dependents, that need to be arranged. When the court names a guardian for your minor children, that named individual might not be the person you would choose to raise your kids, or to receive the benefits of your estate for the purpose of raising them. If you had had the chance to choose, you might have chosen a specific person to raise your children but another specific person to be the trustee over your minor children's estate and Social Security payments.

There may be a proration (who gets how much) of your estate that is being fought over by disgruntled parties--usually those who were left out. If you don't make these types of decisions before you die, your states Intestate laws will make the decisions on your behalf.

The court will appoint an administrator to oversee the many demands of your estate and/or to manage the aspects of your estate. The administrator will be properly bonded inasmuch as he or she is handling someone else's personal funds. A myriad of costs could include, among others, the fees to be bonded, the administrator's fee, the attorney's fees, and other legal and court costs. These will be charged to the estate; all can be potentially expensive and will dilute the ultimate bequest of the heirs.

TESTATE

If, however, you do have a will that is in writing, that is properly dated, executed, witnessed and signed (according to the laws of your state) and it clearly delineates your exact wishes at the time of your death, although a probate or other form of administrative proceeding might still be required, the courts are obligated to respect your wishes. The date on the will is of critical importance in the event that you have created different versions of your will at different times. The most recently dated will (that is properly witnessed and signed) is

---

[4] John W. Reilly. The Language of Real Estate (Illinois: Dearborn Financial Publishing, 2000) p 220

the valid document used to disburse your assets. Make certain that someone always knows about your changes and where the updated will is kept.

In the will you can name the person who you want to be your personal representative who will be responsible for disbursing your assets. Unlike the court-appointed administrator (when you die without a will), you can make your own personal choice in this matter.

In some states the legal term of a personal representative is "executor" because this person "executes" your will and makes certain that your wishes are met. If there is no one individual you particularly trust to perform this task on your behalf, the executor can always be a bank or a trust company.

The choice of a good executor is of paramount importance, especially if your estate might be complicated. The executor needs to be someone who is willing to spend the time needed for the implementation of your will. This person should also understand the legal vagaries of the process in order to minimize potential problems. Assets, such as real property, might need to be sold in order to pay expenses, such as taxes. The executor needs to be given that authority. You might also wish to have your executor bonded, especially if your estate is large and complicated.

How you hold title to your assets (your car, your home, bank accounts, etc.) can make a significant difference as to how those assets will be passed on. If you hold title as "joint tenants," the rest of that title says "with full rights of survivorship." That means, for instance, that if both of you are on the title of your savings account, if one of you dies, the remaining spouse now automatically holds full title to the account. The same thing holds with your home and/or your car--but only if they are held in joint tenancy.

Also, the state in which you are living may have additional laws in how your holdings will be transferred. Your executor may or may not understand these legal vagaries and now would be the time (if not earlier) to confer with an attorney for legal guidance.

Make certain that both husband and wife have their own wills. The husband may die with a will (Testate) that transfers everything to his wife--okay so far. But if the wife dies soon after without a will (Intestate), the probate laws of that state will determine how to distribute what is left. Part of the estate might even go to an ex-spouse, which would definitely not have been either the current husband's or the current wife's wishes!

PROBATE

The only thing the majority of adults know about *probate* is that it should be avoided at all cost. They don't know what probate is or what it does, but what they have heard over the years is that it should be avoided. But hang on--there's more to the story!

All wills (Intestate and Testate) are subject to probate.[5] Probate is where the survivors go to court to prove that the will is valid. Interested parties are informed that the will is being probated, especially any creditors who may need to make a claim against the estate. Depending on the state in which you live and the value of your assets, probate can be an easy, uncomplicated procedure or probate can be a tedious, expensive and long drawn-out process. It just depends.

Probate costs money---there are attorney's fees and court costs. The executor or administrator may need to be bonded, and appraisers may need to be used to determine the value of some of the assets. All of these expenses (including any additional costs such as taxes and outstanding claims) are satisfied (paid) out of the estate. Once the court has been assured that all costs have been paid and sufficient time has passed, the final distribution can be made to the heirs. And the court's decision is usually inviolate--it cannot be challenged.

HOLOGRAPHIC WILL

Many folks think they can avoid the costs of having an attorney draft a will for them and probably having to go to court, by writing the will themselves (holographic). Usually these types of wills are put away in a drawer to be discovered upon the death of the person. There is grave danger in this type of thinking and action. True, the will is in writing and it is probably signed. But if the will doesn't meet the legal standards required by the laws of the state, it could be challenged and declared invalid.

More often than not, these types of wills are imprecise and confusing and end up in court anyway. Some of you readers will be

---

5 Reilly, p 315

old enough to remember the Howard Hughes holographic will in which he left his millions (billions) of dollars to a young man who had picked him up on the highway in the middle of the desert and given him a ride to Las Vegas. The holographic will was contested in court, and the courts finally decided that the will didn't meet the standards required—so the young man got nothing (except sizeable attorney's fees).

In the same vein, if that wayward child who has been disinherited decides to challenge the holographic will in court, the court very well may end up distributing the assets of the estate according to the laws of intestacy—where the probate laws decide who gets what. So even though the person did draft a will indicating who was to get what, the final determination may go against the deceased's wishes. Here is where trying to save a penny can ultimately cost a great deal.

SAFE KEEPING OF THE WILL

Who should keep the will and where should it be kept? In many instances, distribution of the assets can be severely delayed because no-one is able to locate the will and/or other critical papers. As stated above, some people store their wills in a desk drawer or in a filing cabinet in the home.

Sometimes the will is hidden for "safe keeping" behind a picture or under a rug. In some instances, the attorney who helped draft the will keeps either the original or a copy. It doesn't really matter where the original of the will is kept as long as it is safe, someone knows where it is, and it is readily available.

Keeping a copy in a safe-deposit box is a sound idea, but sometimes a safe-deposit box is sealed (by the bank) when the renter of the box dies, which obviously prohibits anyone from immediately accessing the box and retrieving the original will. If someone else's name is on the safe-deposit box as a co-renter, the bank will ordinarily allow that person access, but usually only under close scrutiny. (The bank doesn't want any liability for letting someone retrieve valuables from the box who shouldn't have them.). Just make certain that someone other than yourself knows where the original is being kept.

WHY DO I NEED A LIVING TRUST?

A will is not the only way for you to legally transfer your assets on your death. Another option you can use, that generally requires no probate, is a Living Trust.[6] Because all wills are subject to probate (which can cost money and possibly take several months), it is important for you to know that this other choice is available. *However, it is critical that you consult with an attorney to determine whether, based on your individual circumstances, the best vehicle for you to use is a will or a living trust (or both).* In some states the living trust covers everything that could be covered in a will. In other states, you may still need a will to cover additional assets that the living trust does not.

In the matter of a living trust, your assets and property are held in the trust—provided that is where they have been put. It is a common mistake to establish the trust and then not to transfer the ownership of your assets into the trust. All assets that are held in your name (real and personal property, investments, stocks and bonds, mutual funds, savings accounts, etc.) should be transferred from your name to the name of the living trust. Each partner should have his or her own living trust (but that might vary depending on what your attorney advises).

The name of the trust can be whatever you choose, but in the majority of instances most people choose their own names (the "John Doe Trust," the "Jane Doe Trust," the "Doe Family Trust," etc.). All of your accounts, instead of being in your name, are now in the name of the trust. Forgetting to retitle all your assets into the trust's name will, pretty much, defeat your plans for having established the trust.

REVOCABLE TRUST

You (John Doe) are the trustee of the trust, which means you make all the decisions about how the trust is managed. In some states, joint husband and wife trusts are formed, and both the husband and wife are trustees. As you always did before everything was put into your trust, you maintain the control and you can manage your assets as you always have. You can buy or sell real estate into

---

[6] Nancy Lloyd, "Protect Your Heirs After You're Gone" <u>Parade Magazine</u> 25 February 2001 p 8+

and out of the trust. You can continue to buy and sell your stocks and bonds, and you can continue to put money into and take money out of your checking or savings accounts. The living trust is considered to be a revocable trust, which means that you can change or revoke (cancel) it at any time you wish. As far as you are concerned only the name has changed—except there have been some significant legal changes.

IRREVOCABLE TRUST

Upon your death, your trust immediately becomes *irrevocable* (or, with a joint husband and wife trust, the deceased spouse's share becomes irrevocable). This means that from *that point on* your assets, as the deceased spouse, will be distributed--within a reasonable time-- as you have indicated and spelled out in the trust. In some cases, however, the trust can continue to exist, with your assets being managed and distributed as you have previously decided, even many years after your death. An example of this would be your dictating how funds should be distributed to your children if they are not to receive everything immediately. Is it your intention that the funds should be used many years in the future exclusively for their college education? Should the funds be distributed proportionately, a bit at a time, over many years? At what age should they have total control of the assets? These are examples of how you can control your trust even after your death.

A living trust can direct your wishes concerning children from a previous marriage (that your current spouse might not want to include). You can dictate the long-term care of a child with special needs and/or disabilities, or fund the caretaking of elderly parents. Money can be set aside wherein your ideas cannot be altered.

Except in extenuating circumstances after your death, your decisions are irrevocable. In some states, however, and under some situations, the courts have been known to change the terms of the trust as long as all the beneficiaries agree to it. Use an attorney to make certain the terms of your living trust are as airtight as possible.

CHOOSING A TRUSTEE

As stated earlier, you can be the trustee of your living trust. As the trustee, the trust is entirely in your control and you make all the decisions and changes you wish.

But after your death, just as with an administrator or an executor in a will, someone needs to be named as a "successor trustee" to assure that your wishes are carried out. You (not the court) choose that person. It can be your spouse, a family member you have faith in, or even a bank. If the assets of your living trust are to be distributed even years after your death, far into the future, it would probably be a wise idea to choose an entity such as a bank to be your long-term trustee. Many banks have trust departments who do nothing more than manage other peoples' trusts and assure that the deceased's wishes are carried out, in some cases, over a considerable length of time. Financial institutions, however, generally charge very high trustee's fees that over time may significantly reduce the assets in the trust.

Be careful in choosing your successor trustee. The person (or institution) needs to be someone you can trust implicitly, must have an understanding of the law, must be money savvy, and must be able to devote the time necessary to seeing that your wishes are carried out. It's a time consuming job that deserves to be compensated for.

DIFFERENCES BETWEEN A WILL AND A LIVING TRUST

So why choose a living trust in addition to, or in place of, a will? Although certain notification periods are generally required even when administering a living trust, a trust allows your assets to be distributed to your heirs without the need for going through a possible time-consuming and costly probate. Other than fees that might be paid to a trustee, there are no administrative fees or court costs, so the bulk of your assets goes directly to your heirs and is not diluted in paying other extraneous costs.

A properly drafted living trust can also serve to reduce or eliminate federal estate taxes (sometimes called "death taxes"). And because a living trust is irrevocable after the death of the original trustee, it is harder to contest in a court of law than a will would be. And probably of greatest importance, based on how the living trust is set up, *you can control your assets from the grave.*

And think of this: if you own properties in more than one state, your estate might need to go through probate in each state where you have holdings. This usually can be avoided if your properties are held in a living trust.

Remember that it is up to you to make certain that all the properties you hold are retitled and transferred into the living trust. An attorney can be very helpful and provide invaluable assistance to you in making this happen. But your job will be to get all the information to the attorney.

There may be extenuating personal circumstances that would preclude you from putting your assets in a living trust. *It is imperative that you consult with an attorney and get professional assistance in this matter.*

WHERE THERE'S A WILL (OR A LIVING TRUST) THERE'S A WAY

Setting up a will or a living trust is *not* a do-it-yourself project. Many folks will be tempted to save money and will go online to research the various documents that would seem to satisfy their legal needs. This is a dangerous practice and is extremely risky.

Different states have different laws, and many states require specific legalese or wording in order to make a legal document valid. A generic document pulled off the web could be lacking in these specific state's requirements. You could unwittingly make a mistake and overlook a vital contingency that you want to have carried out. You could misrepresent an issue or your wording could be misinterpreted by those reading it. All these mistakes could ultimately invalidate your wishes.

It is vital that you use an attorney who is experienced in estate planning and can determine what your specific needs and desires are, who can draw up the appropriate legal papers that will assure that your desires and wishes are met, and who can advise you and give you legal counsel and guidance.

If you don't feel that you have the financial resources to consult with an attorney, contact your state's bar association. Many times you can get a consultation with an attorney at no--or little--cost to you. The consultation will not be lengthy, but you can get the legal advice and direction you need to accomplish this extremely important project for your family.

Another advantage to establishing a living trust is that of privacy. A will is a public document, knowledge of which could possibly bring your relatives to the probate hearing--with potentially ugly consequences. The distribution of the assets in the living trust just transpires, without supposedly "interested" parties having access to what is happening.

And remember to readdress your state of affairs periodically, because life's situations change and your mind might change. There are deaths and births, marriages and divorces, changes in opinions and desires. Estate planning is not something that is done once and then forgotten.

The "Five Ds" are a good standard to follow to remind yourself to revisit your decisions: at least every Decade, upon someone's Death, if there is a Divorce, if there has been a serious Diagnosis, and upon a serious Decline.

HEIRLOOMS – PRECIOUS OR PALTRY

Equally as important as cash money someone might inherit, are the precious or paltry heirlooms that are passed on. There have been serious fights and dissentions in families over minor items that have little or no monetary value---all because of the sentimental value they represented to more than one person in the family.[7]

Sisters have gone to war over the rusted tin centerpiece that sat on their mother's kitchen table for 60 years. Brothers have fought over their grandfather's old shaving equipment that both expected to get. Emotions are high, feelings are raw, and as distasteful as it might seem, the mercenary and jealous sensitivities are paramount. And everyone--watch out!

At the very time when the deceased person should be mourned, these types of attitudes serve only to denigrate his or her memory. Old feelings and resentments among siblings and/or cousins can be relived. And when fighting for material possessions, it only brings out the worst in each other.

No-one intends to create divisions in their family and friends on their passing—but can you see how easily it happens? We all expect our kids to act friendly and act like adults. But that might be expecting too much. Our planning can help that to happen.

---

[7] Terry D. Hargrave, Ph.D. "Hard Questions" <u>Modern Maturity Magazine</u>, May/June 2001 p 32

Many folks don't think they have anything of value to pass on—especially thinking of going to the effort of designating who should get particular items. But many times the value is not a dollar value, but a sentimental desire for something. Those desires can be fierce and can bring a lot of jealous pain. Some of the least valuable items can generate the biggest fights. So never assume that no-one will want to have anything that you own.

HOW TO BEGIN?

If it is possible, make a descriptive list of the heirlooms or precious (to you) items that you think there is value in passing on. If there is a story that accompanies the item, make note of that—make the story personal and as accurate as possible. Get the family members together, all at the same time, and discuss the items on the list. If you feel it is appropriate, you may discuss the monetary value of some of the items of interest—provided you know what it is. Some items may be of great enough value to hire a professional appraiser.

You may find that what's important to you, none of your family is interested in---and vice versa. There may be a lot of interest generated in something you would have not thought had any appeal. Now is a great time to talk! Keep the communication open and respectful. Remind everyone that compromise is necessary and that your intention is to be as fair with everyone as you can.

The first thing to do is ASK. Ask your family members to identify what is important to them that they would like to have when you are gone. They can make their own list, they can put a sticker on the item they want (with their name), they can negotiate with others for what they would like to have. But more importantly, they need to let you know what their wishes are. Put everything in writing or you might forget who asked for what when the time comes for you to make your heirloom list with the final designations on it.

Make certain that this heirloom list is readily available when the time comes for the distributions. It won't do any good being tucked away in a book or a drawer and no-one knowing of its existence. Oftentimes a will or living trust will designate the executor or the trustee as the person responsible for overseeing a fair distribution of the personal property. If not, choose someone you trust to see to the fair and equitable disbursal of your valued treasures.

You might consider giving away some of your possessions right now, especially if they are packed away in a box or are somewhere gathering dust. Some of your possessions have a great story that goes along with them. Why not sit down, write a little note giving the history of this treasure, and package everything together creating a really memorable gift. You might as well delight in watching your granddaughter using and enjoying the antique vase that was given to you by your grandmother.

You will quickly discover that there are many, many items left over that no-one has spoken for. Before you die, discuss with your heirs a distribution method that all can agree on. Some families hold an auction on each item with the proceeds from the auction going to a charity or a scholarship—someplace that has been already agreed upon. Some families hold a drawing—from oldest to youngest, then from youngest to oldest.

This procedure might include the entire generations of the family, or, it might begin with just the first generation doing all the choosing. Then at some point, the drawing is turned over to the second or third generations, or maybe to friends.

It obviously doesn't matter what method you use to distribute your possessions, as long as everyone has agreed to it. One of the elder members of your family, particularly someone who has the respect of everyone, can be the person who follows through with the distribution of the possessions.

The important thing to remember is—it's only stuff. Having an intact and loving family is paramount. And it's this type of forward planning, done by you, that will save arguments and bad feelings and will assure the on-going harmony of your posterity for many more years.

Action Items for This Chapter:

(1) If you do not have a living trust or a will, contact your attorney right now.

(2) If you do have a living trust or a will, check the date. When was it last updated? It is suggested that these documents need to be revisited at the "5 Ds"—

    a. Decade

    b. Death

    c. Divorce

    d. Diagnosis

    e. serious Decline

(3) Make a list of your heirlooms, precious or not. Are they hidden somewhere? Is there a story that goes with the heirloom?

CHAPTER THREE

HE SAYS—SHE SAYS
--or--TEACH ME HOW TO SURVIVE IN YOUR WORLD

↩↝

PLEASE REMEMBER – MY GREATEST DESIRE IS TO BE INDEPENDENT---I WANT MOST TO BE ABLE TO DO IT BY MYSELF!

This chapter may seem overwhelming considering the amount of information I suggest that you gather in order to ease your way as a surviving spouse, whether you are a husband or a wife. These issues can easily be overlooked in the minutia of everyday living, but can come critically to the fore upon your spouse's death when you are grieving and laboring to put one foot in front of the other, and now the common aspects of just living add to the daily struggle. You have been left at a critical, excruciating time in your life trying to find these details and trying to learn—the hard way—how and/or where something is, and how it works.

This is the practical information that, upon your partner's death, you will suddenly discover you need a great deal of--right now. In a heightened emotional state, you will have difficulty finding these pieces of information. And what's more—you don't have the energy to try to look for them. Your spouse is gone and is no longer there to answer your questions.

> *May 3/99 – Oh crap! I am in the worst mess. The toilet flooded over and I can't believe I didn't know where the water shut-off valve is to my new "home" (and I use that term loosely)! The carpets are being dried with huge industrial-size fans and, even though they've assured me this is clean water, I can't help but think I need to replace the entire carpet. I can't afford that, but I can't stand the thoughts of it either. Crap! Now I have to worry about this on top of everything else.*

Gathering information now--or, doing as much as you can--can save great amounts of anguish and distress. How much easier the surviving spouse's life will be if these issues have, *at a minimum*, been talked about. Granted, not every spouse deals with some of the issues listed here. These lists are for the purpose of triggering your own thoughts and gathering your own pieces of information for discussion.

In this chapter the husband can take his wife by the hand and walk her through some of the fundamental and practical issues in the daily applications of his life; and she can do the same for him.

My advice to you is to take one evening and make a game out of seeing how much of this material you can gather--between the two of you. By working together the task won't seem as tedious.

I gathered the research for this chapter by asking each new widow or widower I met, "What didn't you know that, upon not having your spouse available to ask a question of, created the most frustrating disruption in your new life?" I got everything from a widower telling me he didn't know the password to his wife's computer, to a wife not knowing where the safe deposit box key was. As for me, I didn't know where the shut-off valve for the water was.

As we have talked about earlier, statistically it is the wife that will be the remaining spouse, so the issues we will first discuss will relate more to a widow than to a widower. So, husbands? Please go through these items with your wife, and those that will pertain to your situation, explain them thoroughly.

And wives? Because trying to learn these things could surely throw you out of your comfort zone, you may persuade yourself that you want to ignore this chapter and go onto the next. Whatever you do, do NOT discourage your husband from teaching you those things you could handle by yourself. And husbands—the same goes for you. The more you know, the better off you will be.

Envision the first time something goes wrong—something your recently deceased spouse would ordinarily have taken care of. And now envision yourself stepping up to the plate and solving the problem without having to call someone else (your son or daughter) for help. If you can do that—it is a proud moment.

Do not allow yourself to be vulnerable to outside influences once you are single. "Vultures" are out there waiting to pounce on your naiveté. You will want to take care of yourself.

FYI--the beginning lists are weighted more heavily toward helping the widows inasmuch as there is, and always will be, a preponderance of widows. There are some items at the end of the chapter that will be focused on helping the widower. The reality of our current lives is that in this day and age many men already do the things women do and vice versa. So you may want to look at the following as being gender-neutral. The lists are lists—nothing more, and they are not necessarily all-inclusive. Use what is provided here to trigger other ideas of your own.

Please recognize that no-one will ever be able to do everything itemized on these lists, nor will you want to. But learning to do as much as you can and as much as you want to—comfortably--will help ease your way as that single person.

SAVING THE WIDOW--HOME MAINTENANCE

When we finally accepted the fact that Gary's illness was terminal, we reluctantly sold our home of twenty-two years and moved into a condominium that was half the size of our home. We did this in order to get me settled into a situation where the exterior (lawns, shrubs, snow removal, etc.) would be maintained, and my only upkeep concern would be the inside of the condo. I was grateful that Gary was as viable as he was and could help me make those decisions that are part of moving. I still have a hard time calling my condo my "home," and I wonder many times if I did the right thing. The move was pretty drastic and many couples would not consider moving from their home to be an option.

An even more drastic move would be into an apartment (unless you are already there); however, if something goes wrong, either on the inside or the outside, you can call the landlord. *[If you are currently living in an apartment, breeze through this section, see if anything applies, then go onto the next section.]*

YARD

Maintaining a yard is not for the faint of heart—it requires a lot of work. But many folks get great pleasure producing a beautiful yard for themselves and for the neighborhood to enjoy. Discuss whether either of you (husband or wife) can do the work alone? Can your wife handle the larger equipment for yard work—does she know how? Or, the biggest question of all---does she want to?

For some folks, the outside yard is an extension of the inside of their home, is very personal space, and they want it to be maintained "just so." Discuss what should be done if all of a sudden, in the middle of the hot summer, the wife is now suddenly dealing with the death of her spouse—and also with the fact that there is watering and mowing to be done.

Following is the first of many sections to get the two of you talking about issues. Use these lists to create your own loose-leaf book and/or computer files with the information you find relevant. And remember, there will be many items that will have no meaning at all to you or your spouse, so work with the ones that do—and add your own.

YARD ISSUES TO DISCUSS
- Running the lawn mower.
- What lawn fertilizer to use, how often and using the fertilizer spreader.
- Running the weed-eater, threading the weed-eater.
- Digging flower beds, if necessary.
- Planting flowers, when and what kind of flowers to plant.
- Watering the flower beds, how often to water.
- What flower fertilizer and/or pesticide to use.
- Turning on and off the sprinkling system.
- Programming and/or adjusting the automatic sprinkling system.

- Draining the outdoor water lines, when to drain, and the location of the outdoor water shut-off valve.
- Location of the manuals and warranties for each piece of outdoor yard equipment.

HEATING/COOLING SYSTEMS

A little education saves a lot of money in being able to not call a professional to do the menial maintenance tasks such as changing a furnace filter or relighting a pilot light. If you don't know what you are doing, however, it is far better to hire the professional than to get yourself in trouble by doing something the wrong way.

Every person needs to know, in an emergency, how to turn off the gas source or the propane source into the home! This is one time when you can't think it is okay to wait around for a professional (or some other person) to come rescue you. This is also not the time (i.e., an earthquake?) to be searching around for something to turn off the valve! Male or female, man or wife, young or old—all need to know where the shut-off valve is and, equally as important, where the wrench is to turn off the valve. The best thing you can do is to have one wrench that is kept by the turn-off valve at all times.

HEAT and COOLING ISSUES TO DISCUSS
  GAS/PROPANE HEAT
- Where is the outdoor gas or propane turn-off and where is the wrench?
- When is the annual maintenance service to be done on the gas/propane furnace?
- What size furnace filters to use.
- Changing the furnace filter and how often.
- Oiling the furnace and how often.
- How often to get the ducts and registers cleaned professionally.
- Adjusting the duct dampers.

- Programming and unprogramming the automatic thermostat.
- Relighting a pilot light.
- Who to call for professional service and what is the phone number?

ELECTRIC HEAT
- When is the annual maintenance service to be done on the electric heating system?
- Programming and unprogramming the automatic thermostat.
- Who to call for professional service and what is the phone number?

AIR-CONDITIONING
- When is the annual maintenance service to be done on the central air conditioning?
- Maintaining a swamp cooler with a water line.
- Changing filters in a swamp cooler.
- Covering a swamp cooler at the end of the season.
- Who to call for professional service and what is the phone number?

PLUMBING

As mentioned in a previous chapter, not knowing where the indoor valve was to turn off the water (and stop my toilet from flooding over) was the beginning of my knowing that I didn't know very much. Plumbing issues are like most other maintenance issues—for most of them it is best to call for a professional. But there are a few things that can be easily learned and readily and cheaply remedied. And, remember--a leaky faucet can waste a lot of precious water if it's not repaired, either by you or someone else, in a timely fashion.

PLUMBING ISSUES TO DISCUSS
- Where is the water turn-off valve inside the house?
- Stopping a toilet from flooding over until the plumber can come.

- Changing a washer in a leaky water faucet.
- Maintaining a septic tank.
- Who to call for professional service and what is the phone number?

WATER HEATER
- Resetting the thermostat on the water heater.
- Draining the water heater and how often.
- When should the water heater be replaced?
- Relighting the pilot light.
- Who to call for professional service and what is the phone number?

ELECTRICAL

Electrical issues are the same as plumbing issues—you don't want to fool too much with them. But there are a few simple things that are easy to understand and can save you from having to call a professional.

A fuse box or an electric service panel function the same: both house and control the electricity coming in from the outside. The fuses in a fuse box will "blow," or the circuit breakers in a service panel will "trip" (they are designed to turn off the power) if there is a surge of power in that particular area of the electric service box.

If there is suddenly no power in one particular area of the house, you can go to the service box, identify the problem, and replace the fuse or reset the breaker switch. Know what to do if there is an overload--too many appliances plugged into one circuit. Unplug all the appliances, reset the breaker (or put in a new fuse), then add back the appliances one at a time. Know how to reset a GFI outlet if it trips.

ELECTRICAL ISSUES TO DISCUSS
- Where is the electric service panel?
- Are all the areas clearly labeled?
- Discovering a tripped breaker switch and how to reset it.
- Discovering a blown fuse and how to replace it.

- Resetting a tripped GFI outlet.
- Who to call for professional service and what is the phone number?

APPLIANCES/ELECTRONIC EQUIPMENT

When something doesn't work, always check first the electric service panel and make certain the circuit breakers or fuses are okay. Restore electricity if necessary. Trying to repair an appliance may work or not, depending on what the problem is. Having retained the warranties and the manuals for each appliance, tool, and/or small machine that you have purchased may prove to be extremely beneficial. Store all manuals in one accessible location

Get out the manual when something goes wrong with an appliance. In almost all cases, the manual will have a section on "troubleshooting" and will give step by step instructions as to how to make a repair. If that doesn't work, you have at least tried. The next thing to do is to call the repairman.

Sometimes the repair of small appliances is more tedious than purchasing new. You will make that choice.

Where is the manual and warranty for each of the following (why not store them in the same place?):

LARGE APPLIANCE ISSUES TO DISCUSS
- refrigerator
- freezer
- stove or stove top
- oven
- microwave
- dishwasher
- garbage disposal
- trash compactor
- washing machine
- clothes dryer
- hot water heater
- air conditioner/swamp cooler
- furnace
- other_____

Where is the manual and warranty for each of the following:

SMALL APPLIANCE ISSUES TO DISCUSS

- electric tool (drill, etc.)
- TV, VCR/DVD
- computer/printer/scanner/copier
- other_____

    _____

MISCELLANEOUS MAINTENANCE

Until there is a serious problem, some aspects of home maintenance don't get recognized (mostly by the widow) and taken care of on a timely basis—for instance, exterior painting. Unaccustomed to watching out for these kinds of issues, and/or concerned that there is not enough money to fix anything, the widow tends to let the matter go until it is truly problematic. Establishing some kind of maintenance schedule for the survivor can help in solving these kinds of problems.

I was determined to build a couple of shelves by myself: one under my bathroom sink, another in my linen closet. I hate to admit that I couldn't remember how to put the head of the screwdriver in the power drill, so I ended up screwing in the brackets using my own power. I measured for the shelves, measured again, and measured a third time—then had a friend cut the shelves for me. They are a sad sight to see, but they have lasted—and I built them by myself!

MAINTENANCE ISSUES TO DISCUSS

- When was the roof last replaced?
- Is there a schedule for painting either the inside or the outside?
- What paint is used for the outside trims, what color do you use?
- Cleaning the rain gutters and when.
- Opening the garage door if there is no power or if it is broken.
- Who to call for a reputable, honest handyman and what is the phone number?

SECURITY

When thinking of home security, most people think of a professional home security system with an alarm that alerts the police (or someone else) if there is a break-in while the owner is gone from home. But home security can mean many more things, such as: fire alarms, smoke detectors, carbon monoxide detectors, personal health monitors, deadbolts on doors and windows, outside lights, a barking dog, etc. Feeling safe in one's home is paramount to one's peace of mind.

SECURITY ISSUES TO DISCUSS

- What company monitors and services your alarm and what is their number?
- Setting and unsetting the security alarm.
- What does the security system provide: theft, fire, personal health monitor, anything else?
- What to do if the alarm sounds.
- Setting the alarm for security while you are inside.
- Where is the security alarm paper work and warranties?
- What is the security password?

AUTOMOBILE(S)

For the widow, automobile maintenance is probably more challenging than the maintenance of the home. Many women will report that when they walk into an automobile mechanic's shop they feel as defenseless as though they have a bulls-eye on their front— "hit me with what you have because I have no clue." They are just waiting to be taken advantage of by an unscrupulous mechanic. Mechanics can throw out unfamiliar terms such as: drive shaft, deferential, tire rod, generator, combustion, and--what does she know?

Helping your wife to find a reputable, reasonably priced, *honest* car mechanic can be one of the most caring and thoughtful things you can do for her. It's not that she will only be saving money, it's more the fact that she can trust in this person when she feels particularly vulnerable.

69

When Gary was no longer driving his truck, it was evident that I would have to sell it. But it seemed like such a betrayal for me to sell it while he was still alive. Someone suggested to us that it could expedite my selling the truck if he were to sign (and have notarized) the title over to me—which he did. That facilitated my selling it a few months later to a teenager and his dad who negotiated my price down to $750. I knew I had it priced right, but I had no fight in me and let it go for what they offered. I'm still mad at myself for doing that.

Locate the following information for each automobile that is in your family.

AUTOMOBILE ISSUES TO DISCUSS
- Oil change - how often to change, grade/brand of oil.
- Where is the sticker that reminds you of the oil change?
- Do you need to get the emissions checked, how often and where?
- Where are the car service and maintenance records?
- Tires—what size, when to rotate, when to purchase.
- Insurance – what company, name of agent, phone number.
- Where is the automobile insurance policy?
- Registration – how to register the car, how often.
- Where to purchase a new car, from whom and a phone number.
- Location of VIN (vehicle identification number).
- Who to call for a reputable, honest auto mechanic and what is the phone number?

And last but not least: how do you change a tire?

BOATS, RECREATIONAL VEHICLES, MOTOR HOMES, PLANES

Not too many of us have the luxury of having any of the above, but if you do, you need to complete the same exercises as you have just finished with the automobiles. Maintenance requires the same procedures; insurance is similar, registration is similar. As a surviving spouse, if it becomes necessary to sell one of the above, having all the information readily available will be an advantage.

Can't you just gather all the paperwork at a later time? Of course you can. But if you are still suffering and grieving the loss of your spouse, can you understand how your way can be eased if you already have this information at your fingertips?

MISCELLANEOUS—THIS AND THAT

Over the years I have accumulated lists and more lists of a variety of things that should be discussed between the spouses. There seems to be no specific category in which to place these items, so I have called the category "THIS and THAT." These items identify frustrations of the widows and widowers I have interviewed when I asked them what they wished they had known.

For those in the baby boom generations and older, almost universally, the wife did not know how to pay the monthly bills. But worse than that, it was she who had resisted learning how when her husband tried to teach her. Or, perhaps, she knew how to pay the simple monthly charges such as the utility bills and the grocery bills, but had refused to pay anything more complicated than that, such as credit card bills, mortgage payments, etc. Now she was suddenly a widow, and now she was having to call on her children to help her. And not surprisingly, she was unable to answer their questions so that they *could* assist her.

I had a minor difficulty getting into our safe deposit box after Gary's death even though I was signatory on the box and also had the key. Obviously the bank does not want someone getting into the box and cleaning out valuables and/or money before there has been a legal accounting and/or distribution of the assets via either a living trust or probate. If you *don't* have a key and your signature is not on the card, it's even harder to get in. Some banks are more flexible than others, and sometimes if the bank has a copy of the death certificate and you can provide proper identification, the safe deposit box can be drilled open.

I must confess that there was one thing Gary tried to teach me that just didn't take. I should have been able to learn it and I just couldn't--how to change the time on my watch. Living in a state that utilizes daylight savings time has been a nightmare for me every six months. But I have solved the problem. I have two identical

71

watches: one on regular time and one on daylight savings time. When the time comes, I just switch watches. Hey—it works for me!

The problem with all these lists is that sometimes you don't know what you don't know—so how can you ask questions and try to get answers if you don't know what information you need? Hopefully going through the following items will trigger other questions you also need answers to:

THIS AND THAT ISSUES TO DISCUSS
- Location of the safe-deposit box(es).
- Location of the key(s) to the safe-deposit box(es).
- Am I signatory on the safe-deposit box(es)?
- What is in the safe-deposit box(es)?
- What is the password on my spouse's computer?
- What is the combination on my spouse's briefcase?
- How do I program the VCR/DVD?
- How do I change the time on my watch?
- Location of the storage unit(s).
- Location of the key(s) to the storage unit.
- What is in the storage unit(s)?
- When does the trash go out?
- How and when to pay the monthly bills, filing important papers.
- What papers should be filed, what papers should be trashed?
- Identify all the loose keys in all the drawers and label them.
- Make duplicate sets of keys to the house, car and boat.
- What is the combination to the home safe?
- What is in the home safe?
- Location of the key to the gun safe.
- Location of licenses to carry a gun.

SAVING THE WIDOWER

As has already been noted, statistics prove that a large percentage of widowers don't survive the first year of their spouse's death.

Loneliness is obviously a huge factor, but what about the fact that the widower has never learned to take care of himself? This is the opportune time for a wife to lead her husband through the following items and tasks and help educate him in how to take care of himself if she is gone.

Make certain you both know where the appliance manuals are. These can be of great help in advising you to the cleaning and maintenance of the appliance(s), and some manuals even have recipes.

COOKING
- How do you cook more than an egg or a frozen dinner for yourself.
- Cooking a roast in the oven.
- Using the broiler.
- Using a crockpot.

STOVE-TOP or OVEN
- Using what pans with which stovetop units.
- Lighting a gas stovetop unit.
- Pulling out the stovetop units and cleaning them.
- Cleaning the oven using the self-clean feature (use no other method).
- Cleaning the oven using an oven cleaner (if there is no self-clean feature).

MICROWAVE
- Using the microwave—no pans or dishes with metal or metallic trim.
- Identifying a microwavable dish.
- Cleaning the interior – no abrasive cleaners or scouring pads.

REFRIGERATOR
- Storing perishables?
- Packing the freezer with frozen food.
- How often to clean the refrigerator (check manual).
- Cleaning the interior shelves and gaskets.
- Vacuuming coils on back or underneath (check manual).

DISHWASHER

- Don't let dishes block spray-arm.
- Cleaning the interior (check manual).
- What dishwasher soap to use.
- Avoiding spots on dishes.
- Other_____

GARBAGE DISPOSAL

- Let cold water run freely for at least a minute after you finish grinding.
- Using the wooden end of a broom stick to unjam a jammed disposal.
- Where the reset button is.
- Grinding lemon rinds to freshen the smell.

GROCERY SHOPPING

- Shopping the perimeter of the store.
- Taking a shopping list.
- Picking produce and meat.
- Looking for expirations dates (especially on dairy).
- Reading product labels.
- Using coupons.

LAUNDRY

- Separating darks from whites.
- Pre-treating stains.
- What detergent to use.
- What water cycle to use/what temperature to use.
- Using bleach, or, how to get whites "tidy-whitey".
- Cleaning the lint screen and how often.
- Balancing the washing machine (turn legs clockwise to lower them or counterclockwise to raise them - (check manual).
- Ironing fronts, collars and cuffs of a cotton shirt.
- Cleaning the bottom of a dirty iron.
- Other_____

CLEANING THE HOUSE
- Pros and cons of using cleaning ladies or a cleaning service.
- What is the schedule for cleaning which rooms, or, is there a schedule?
- Recognizing which items need attention.
- Deciding which problems can be ignored for a while.
- Paying attention to the corners, wherever they may be.
- What cleaning products to use on which items.
- Hiring out a task to be done.
- Watering the indoor plants and how often--what fertilizer to use.
- Caring for the pet(s).
- Cleaning up after the pet(s).

Gathering this information doesn't have to happen all at once. But while you have the momentum, do as much as you can. You will find that while you are looking for one item, you may easily find other item(s) nearby (e.g., appliance manuals all in the same file). Have an idea of what items you need to be looking for. Take advantage of what you have already found in certain files and you may locate something else.

It should be obvious by now that not everything on these lists is going to pertain to everyone. Take what is meaningful and valuable to you, and ignore the rest. If it sometimes feels as though you are being fed with a fire hose as you progress through this chapter, just let go of what has no meaning to you.

Should you use this chapter as a "workbook," checking off items as you find them? Whatever it takes. It doesn't matter how you do it—only that you do it.

PLEASE REMEMBER – I MOST WANT TO BE ABLE TO:
(1) do it by myself, (2) easily ask someone to do it for me, and, when all else fails, (3) pay someone to do it for me.

Action Items for This Chapter:

(1) Sign off ten items in this chapter each day--you will be done in about two weeks.

(2) Do the simplest items first—make great headway at the very beginning and, who knows, you will probably be finished in less than two weeks.

(3) You don't need to complete every single item—just those that you know will be important to your spouse when you are no longer there to help.

CHAPTER FOUR

REST EASY
--or--PLANNING YOUR FUNERAL

〜

PRE-ARRANGEMENT

As with all the other preparedness items in this book, preplanning your funeral provides guidance and direction to those left behind. On the surface this seems like a morbid thought—here again, because you are discussing end-of-life issues.

But if both you and your partner are still vibrant and in good health and can be fairly pragmatic about the process, strange as it may appear at first, once you get started it can be a surprisingly positive experience. As a matter of fact, it can be quite rewarding.

Many people come away feeling grateful for the control they have had in making these major decisions for the end of their lives. Each partner knows exactly what the other wants because each has had the opportunity to discuss personal preferences, wishes and needs. When you are *not* burdened with an illness or unfavorable circumstances, you can make your decisions with clear and unencumbered thinking. If you are suddenly thrust into making funeral plans for your partner when you are under duress and in a fragile emotional condition, this is a precarious time to be making decisions. The death of your loved one can bring an unbelievable amount of stress, confusion and grief, and if the grief is coupled with uncertainty or guilt, it is easy to make rash unwise decisions.

Now is not the time to be staging a grand funeral production in order to prove your love. If you are feeling guilty over something bad that has happened during your married lifetime, now is not the time to want to make amends by purchasing an expensive and unnecessary funeral package. The deceased spouse won't know and won't care.

A sudden and unexpected death does not provide for a planning period because everything is happening quickly and decisions need to be made right now. Preplanning can free your partner from making pressured and unnecessary decisions at a most vulnerable time. Your family can be saved from unnecessary pain and expense by having all the decisions made and, in some situations, having the financial obligations completely paid. Those who are remaining will have no deadline pressures.

With pre-planning, cooler heads can prevail and make more intelligent choices with more personal decisions and wishes being carried out. This is probably the most rewarding aspect of making your own plans while you are able to think--and plan--clearly. If you have a particular penchant for something special in your life (e.g., cowboy, musician, automobile mechanic, photographer, hunter, etc.) you can choose to have the specialty recognized at your life's end. It's all about you making your own decisions.

Probably the hardest thing to do is making the appointment to go to the funeral home to begin the process. Remember that old word—PROCRASTINATION? Here again, you want to do it, you know you should do it, you intend to do it. So, why don't you?

Experienced and professional people are there to help you choose and decide exactly what your own wishes are. They will take you through the process and help you to write an end to your life's story that is told in your way and your way only. Once you have completed the process, you are done. You will leave feeling amazingly free and unburdened.

CHOOSING YOUR FUNERAL PROVIDER

Most folks don't give too much thought to what funeral provider they want to use. In most cases, they choose a provider either by (1) location, (2) family history, or (3) personal recommendation.[8]

Think about it: immediately after the death of a loved one is not the time that you are in the emotional state to go bargain hunting. All you want is to be given answers to your problems. Where am I supposed to go? What am I supposed to be doing? I have never done this before—who can I rely on to steer me the right path?

You will probably choose the path of least resistance—someplace you can feel comfortable either because of previous experience, a convenient location, or the funeral home has been referred to you by someone you trust.

All of that is important, but if you are not allowed the time to deliberately choose your provider, you may be setting yourself up for additional costs and services that you might have been able to avoid.

If you have the opportunity to shop around when you can make unemotional choices, you will be in a sounder position when the real "time" comes. At the least, call several funeral homes and request an itemized price list to be sent to you. You can begin by reviewing prices and services.

FINANCIAL DECISIONS

The high costs of a funeral are nearly always a surprise. For that reason it is to your advantage to make these decisions while you can look at options and tailor your end-of-life wishes to those that can fit your budget and also lessen the burden on your survivors.

---

[8] Erika Rasmusson and Janes Lisa Scherzer "10 Things Funeral Directors Won't Tell You" SmartMoney.com 28 June 2010

By pre-planning, you can make the decisions yourself as to how much money you want to spend for a funeral package. You can determine the budget yourself, maybe cutting corners in one area and splurging a little more in another. You can look at the General Price List (GPL) and decide just what looks good to you. What items you want to include, and what items you choose to discard.

You can either pre-pay for what you want in a lump sum, or you can make arrangements for paying when and how it is convenient for you.

Some people look on prearrangement as being sound financial planning, because you are buying your services on today's dollar. If you live for ten to twenty (or more) years, you can readily see what a sound investment that could be.

Obviously, you will want to do your preplanning with a funeral home that has been in the community for a long time and you know has a sound reputation. If you make your plans today, and you don't die for another twenty years, will your provider still be around? Will your money still be available to pay for your costs and services?

A question that you will want to ask of the funeral director is— where does your money go when you prepay for your own funeral? You want to make certain the money can't be absconded by the director (or someone else) and diverted to other areas.

In most cases, to be safe, the money should either purchase an insurance policy (to be paid on your death), or it should be put into a trust account. Make certain either the policy or the account is in your name and not that of the funeral home, only.

FUNERAL COSTS

So how much does a funeral cost? One can hear averages for an adult funeral from $2800 up to $28,000, depending on your location. Funeral costs average higher in the eastern states than in the western states, but there are still many variables that can push the costs into the stratosphere.

Statistics from the National Funeral Directors Association (NFDA) indicates that the average cost of an adult funeral increases with each passing year. (This survey is not conducted annually; 2009 is the most recent year for which NFDA has data.) [9]

Year	Cost of an Adult Funeral
1991	$3742
1995	$4626
2000	$5180
2006	$6195
2009	$6560

Inflation obviously affects the costs of a funeral. Buying a funeral plan on today's dollar makes sound financial sense.

The best part of all is that your spouse or your children will not have the pressure of raising large sums of money when all they should be doing at this time is grieving. Can you imagine how relieved your survivors will be when they realize that all, or at least most, of your funeral arrangements have been paid? And, if this has been taken care of, the money received from life insurance benefits can go into the survivor's estate and not be depleted by funeral costs.

Similar to choices made at a wedding, the individual services one selects can add to the tally. Some of the funeral services are required by law, but others can be of your own choice.

Services differ from state to state and from funeral home to funeral home, but they may include the following:

- *Professional services* – Costs for the professional staff that serves your needs including the funeral director, secretaries, drivers, flower arrangers, etc.
- *Embalming/Cremation* –In most cases, if the deceased is going to be cremated, embalming is not necessary providing the cremation happens very shortly after death. In other cases, and depending on the particular state, embalming is required by law. (More about this later.)
- *Other preparations* –The preparation of the body so that it can be viewed by friends and family, which can include cosmetics, dressing the body, fixing the hair.

[9] 2010 NFDA General Price List Survey. Retrieved 5 Feb 2013 from www.nfda.org/media:center/statisticsreports.html

- *Visitation/viewing* – The cost can differ depending on the number of days the body will be viewed. Customs vary from state to state. In some states, visitation can last many days; in other states visitation is limited to just prior to the funeral.
- *Funeral at the funeral home* – Costs include the use of the facilities of the funeral home, staff to facilitate the guests at the funeral, staff for accommodating the flowers, staff that will provide music or other parts of the service, etc.
- *Funeral home transferring* – This cost is usually part of the basic services and it includes the receiving of the deceased at the place of death—home, hospital, rest home, or wherever-- and transferring the remains to the funeral home or to some other place.
- *Hearse (or coach)* – The cost of transporting the casket to the place of the funeral then to the place of burial.
- *Service car/van* – A limousine and/or van will transport the immediate family, and the utility vehicle will transport the flowers.
- *Memorial acknowledgements* – Includes the guest register book and other items to memorialize the deceased. The mortuary can provide the "thank you" cards for the survivors to acknowledge flowers or condolences from the guests.
- *Casket* – The greatest variance in price for the entire funeral arrangement will be the cost of the casket. In some cases, the funeral home will give one blanket cost (based on the cost of the casket) that will include all, or most, of the above services.
- *Urn* - Includes the purchase of a container in which to place the deceased's cremated remains.
- *Vault* – The cement liner that is usually not required by law, but may be required by the cemetery in which the burial is to take place.

Since the Funeral Rule of 1984 that was put in place by the Federal Trade Commission, the individual costs for all the above services must be disclosed to you in what is called "a funeral cost estimate" or a GPL (General Price List). This allows you to see, line item by line item, exactly what you will be paying for---what is mandated by law and what is an option for you to purchase. You have the opportunity to make financial adjustments in what you want and/or need, and what you can do without. This is the time that you can eliminate any services you decide you don't need or want--as long as the service isn't required by law.

> *March 3/99 - We went looking for caskets this afternoon. What a mind boggling experience it was. I'm glad I've gone through this before with Mother and Mom Post, but nonetheless, it's really nerve wracking. The funeral home provides everything for the price of the casket so it was a matter of finding one that we could afford. There was a very pretty knotty-pine that I think Gary would have chosen for himself, but all I could think of was what others might think--that we were putting him in knotty-pine.*

The retail mark-up on caskets is fairly significant and can be as much as 100% for personalization.[10] Discount caskets can be purchased from a variety of places such as Costco or Wal-Mart, and the funeral home is required to use the casket you have purchased. But recognize that for the funeral home to cover its own expenditures, some of the costs for the other services you have chosen may have to be increased. But all of that will be clearly disclosed to you.

In many cases you will be offered a package price that includes most of the items you want for a reduced price.

OBITUARY

Probably the hardest thing for family members to do is to write your obituary--especially if they don't know (or can't remember) all that you have done in your life. What would you like your obituary to say? Do you want it to identify all your accomplishments, or do you

---

[10] CNBC TV Special Report "Death: It's a Living" 31 January 2013.

want to keep it short and simple and be just a notification of your death—or something in between?

Better yet, why don't you write your own obituary? Is that too morbid? Think about it. This way you can say exactly what you want to say and in the way you want it to be said. It can be your goodbye to the world. It can spell out what you have done to leave the world a better place. It can be the tribute to yourself that you deserve. And it will be accurate because you wrote it.

Is it wrong to want to "toot your own horn?" Absolutely not! There may be something you would like the world to know about you that can only be said by you. By writing your own obituary you can say those special things that someone else might not think of as being that important.

But remember: most papers will have a per/line charge (plus a picture), so if you get too "wordy" it can be quite costly. So don't give thanks to all your school teachers or list the names of all the animals you owned during your lifetime. But make it memorable.

EMBALMING vs. CREMATION

EMBALMING

Embalming is sometimes a controversial issue between the family (who don't want to have it) and the funeral home (who are advising it be done). States' laws differ requiring embalming, but usually embalming is only required when there is a prolonged time between death and burial (refrigeration can extend this time), when there is to be a public viewing, or if the death has been caused by an infectious disease.

The funeral home professionals are cognizant of the feelings and emotions of those who are left behind and who are making the decisions. They know and understand that when the family sees the body for the first time after the death, that it should look its best. Because of this they might recommend that the body be embalmed. From personal experience, however, and after the passing of my sister, my family and I were able to view her body three days after she had died, and she was absolutely beautiful—with no embalming.

Under ordinary situations the funeral directors will try to accommodate the family's wishes, but there may be extenuating circumstances where it's best for the family to listen to the professionals.

CREMATION

Across the world, cremation has been a standard of burial for centuries--but not as much in the western world. In the United States, however, more and more are choosing to have cremation for themselves or for family members. In 2008 cremations in the United States equaled 36.2%, rising to 42.2% in 2011, with the figure projected for 2025 to reach almost 60%. According to the NFDA, in 2010 the three highest states choosing cremation were Nevada (73%), Washington (71%) and Oregon (69%).[11]

Attitudes over cremation have been changing steadily for many years. Cremation is no longer thought of as barbaric or as a second-world answer to overpopulation. Religious restrictions are easing and cremation seems to be the comfortable answer for more and more people.

Part of that answer could have to do with the significantly reduced cost as compared to a full-service funeral plan. If the deceased is to be cremated immediately there are no embalming costs, no costs for a casket, no costs for the preparation of the body for a viewing. There are significant savings in opting for cremation.

But remember--a quick disposition of the corpse does not make for a quick disposition of pain or grief for the survivors. Even if the body is cremated, there still needs to be a time that is set aside for saying goodbyes and for sharing memories. Ceremonies or rituals of some kind have been used by most cultures for thousands of years as a way for the living to see off the dead—to affirm to the survivors the changed status of their lives forever more. Even after having a

---

[11] Retrieved 5 Feb 2013 from www.nfda.org/media-center/statisticsreports.html also Cremation Association of North America

cremation, most families will still choose to have a memorial service of some kind. Some might choose to have a simple gathering of friends for drinks or a meal where the deceased is remembered. Or some may choose a full funeral service.

There are also varying ideas and attitudes as to what to do with the cremated remains. The ashes can be placed in a beautiful urn customized to the deceased's personality. The urn can then either be buried or can be kept in the household or some other special place of remembrance. A fairly recent option is to place the urn at the bottom of the ocean where corals and sponges will grow over it creating a permanent, very quiet, resting place. And if your family scuba dives, they can even come visit you.

Some will opt to have the ashes scattered over a place that holds a specific memory for the deceased or the deceased's family. Ashes can be exploded as fireworks, loaded into shotgun shells and shot someplace memorable, and even used as paint in artwork.[12]

Or sometimes part of the ashes are scattered and part are kept. Bear in mind, however, that in most states the scattering of ashes is illegal and you may need to get special permission from the authorities to do so.

A good friend of mine, decided she wanted to be cremated and have her ashes spread from an airplane over the Salmon River. She said, "I've always wanted to sky-dive, and now I can." And she did!

Scattering the ashes is a personal choice, but in some cases the survivors end up being disappointed that they then have no place to visit (such as a cemetery) to remember and feel close to the deceased. Burying the ashes in a specific location gives that final sense of "closure" that is sometimes needed by the survivors.

Even though cremation is the family's choice, some will still choose to have the body embalmed, have a viewing and a full funeral service, and then have the body cremated. Of course there will now be many of the same original costs, such as the need for a casket, the

[12]Josh Sandburn, "New American Way of Death" Time Magazine 24 June 2013

preparation of the body for viewing, etc. For many families, however, this is a necessary way to grieve and to say goodbye.

If this is your desire, ask the funeral director if there is the option of renting a casket--with a liner--for the viewing, and a simple cardboard box (or something similar) for the cremation. This would significantly alleviate that one expensive cost. Or, in some instances, the funeral home will have very attractive cardboard caskets that are quite striking and don't have the same sticker shock as a regular casket.

If you want to be cremated, let your family know--in writing. As with organ donation (see CHAPTER FIVE), this is a very personal choice with which others in your family might not agree. And unless everyone in the family does agree, if it is not in writing, some states will not allow for your wishes to be fulfilled.

In preplanning your end-of-life wishes with the funeral home, you will be creating a written memorial guide that will specify your wishes. Upon your death, the funeral director will share this memorial guide with your family which can help alleviate their questions and concerns.

VISITATION/VIEWING

The viewing/visitation is a peaceful, informal time for the family and friends to spend some last moments saying goodbye to their dear one. It's also a time for guests to provide friendship and comfort to the surviving partner and family. When others come to convey their sorrow and to pay their last respects, the family is consoled and reassured by the sympathy and words of comfort that are expressed.

Psychologists tell us that when the immediate family members have a separate, one-on-one time with the deceased in order to say their quiet goodbyes, that the separation and the grieving can be minimized. The presentation of the body is important so that the family can remember the deceased in a positive way. For an extended viewing, the funeral director will strongly support the idea of having the body embalmed. Another expense will be the cost of "beautifying" the body: the cosmetics, hair style and/or cut, the opted-for clothing.

> *March 5/99 – I got to the funeral home way early for the viewing. I wanted to spend some time alone with Gary and settle my thoughts. As I walked over to the casket I could see that his hair was all wrong. It was slicked back and was awful. I tried to fix it myself, but it was plastered with hair spray and wouldn't budge. All my thoughts of reverie were shot to heck as I was trying to find someone who could come fix his hair. They came and got it fixed, but by that time the kids were starting to come. I was wondering about the grandkids and how they would accept seeing their grandpa this way. I watched as they would go over to the casket and just look at Gary—then they would turn around and go play with their cousins. It seemed to be very healthy to me.*

You can make the choice whether to have an open casket or not. If you don't wish to be "viewed" by other than family and close friends, perhaps a favorite picture of yours can sit on the top of the casket or on a table nearby.

You can choose what clothes you would like to be buried in. If you choose to be buried in your wedding dress that's okay, because all they do is split it down the back and, voila, it fits!

Do you want to be wearing your glasses, or your wedding ring? What about your watch? If not, to whom should they go?

Is there anything important to you that you would like to have put in your casket? What about your golf club, your knitting needles, your fishing rod, etc.? Sometimes family members like to place notes or other small and memorable items in the casket as a way of saying goodbye.

FUNERAL SERVICE/CEREMONY

When the end of life comes, almost always there is a ceremony that celebrates that life and says "farewell". There are those who would argue that the ceremony is not necessary—that a swift goodbye and burial is all that is needed.

But evidence suggests that the funeral ceremony provides the utmost of support and healing for those left behind. Through this formal observance and ritual, the survivor begins to recognize and accept that the old life is gone, and that the new life is beginning.

The funeral service is for the survivors, but it is also your "send-off" to wherever you believe you are going. This service is where family and guests meet to listen to stories about you (good or bad), usually have a good laugh and/or a good cry, and where everyone gathers to support the family in its loss. Having the chance to "relive" a life well-lived is comforting to your family and guests. And, if your spiritual belief is that you are going to a new and better place, this belief can be part of the service and can give great strength and peace to your survivors.

Where would you like to hold this memorial ceremony? If you are a religious person you might have a particular house of worship in mind. If not, almost all of the funeral homes have a large, chapel-like room in which to hold a non-sectarian service. Depending on the anticipated size of mourners, there may be large enough rooms in a fraternal lodge, a restaurant, a place of business. You can make that decision.

Now is the chance for you to design your ceremony--to create a farewell event that can reflect upon you and who you were. This is the time to let who you are—or were—shine. You can choose talks, music, demonstrations, videos--anything that lets the family and guests be reminded of their special relationship with you and who you were. Do you have any hobbies you would like to display, any items unique to your profession, any items that magnify your personality and your interests? A demonstration of your pursuits in life can let survivors know and appreciate you as an exceptional and unique individual.

March 6/99 - The funeral was wonderful—quite unusual. Gary played at his own funeral. When he was in the Symphony he played the English horn solo in the second movement of the Dvorak "New World Symphony

89

--it is the plaintive "Going Home" melody that almost everyone knows. We played the tape of his playing that movement and it was mesmerizing.

What kind of music would you like to have? Do you have specific musicians in mind you would like to have play or sing, or do you have a special tape or CD you would like to have played? Would you like the congregation to sing a song or a hymn or two—and what would they be?

Who do you want to conduct or lead the service, and who would you like to speak? Or would you like to have extemporaneous speakers from the congregation?

Whatever you end up choosing, be courteous to your guests and don't plan a program that will take longer than one hour. Your guests will begin to leave, especially if your funeral takes place on a work day.

Having these plans already made can, here again, save your loved ones from having to make the decisions as to what they *think* you would want. This is the time to celebrate your life—let everyone know what you want to do and how you want to do it.

March 6/99 – Dao, the husband of our Vietnamese daughter, Thuy, had recognized the date of Gary's death as being the same date as the day when the people of Vietnam release birds into the air as a way of releasing the spirits to commune with God. Several birds were intermingled with the flower-spray on the coffin,

BURIAL

Do you have a burial plot, or do you wish to be interred in a mausoleum or a lawn crypt? A place of burial is something you obviously need to have, so why not purchase a spot now? Do you have a particular cemetery in mind? If your choice is to be cremated, where do you want your ashes?

Cemetery issues can differ so you must consult the cemetery to find out the specific provisions, rights and exclusions if you are buying or selling your burial plot.

Sometimes there is a family plot with many burial sites already paid for. This might be an option, or you might make the decision to be buried somewhere else (maybe you don't want to be too close to family).

Two or three urns with cremated remains can be buried in one burial plot, or if the cemetery will allow it, one casket can be buried on top of another casket--thereby taking up one plot.

What are your ownership rights with a burial plot? You are not buying a piece of real estate—you are purchasing a property right—best described as an easement or a license to use. You are subject to the laws of the state and the rules of the cemetery as to how you can use your plot. You will either need to know what those regulations are, or your funeral director can guide you in that area.

As cemeteries are filling up, many are now charging an extra fee for a "non-residence" status. In other words, if you do not live in the actual area of the cemetery, you may be charged extra for the plot. And there are differences in the costs of being buried in a public cemetery vs. a private cemetery.

In some cemeteries grave markers (headstones) must be flat in the ground. Others may carry a fee that covers "perpetual care" where special maintenance is required.

If an owner of an unused burial plot dies Intestate (without a will), the plot will pass to his or her heirs in the same manner other property passes in the absence of a will (it will go through probate along with the rest of the deceased's estate).

GRAVESIDE SERVICE

In most cases, only very close family and friends come to the graveside service. If the family chooses, there can be a prayer dedicating the grave as a place of peace and rest. There may be a military honor guard at this time or there may be other participating organizations (such as a lodge or a union) that will pay last respects. This is one more opportunity for the family to have greater "closure" and acceptance.

Sometimes the graveside service is the only service that is held for the deceased. For a variety of reasons that is the family's choice. Or that might have been your own personal choice. There can be speakers and/or music, but because most of the attendees will be standing, the service is usually quite short.

In a few months after the ground has settled around the gravesite, a marker (headstone) can be placed. You can design your own marker. What would you like it to say? Are there some final words of wisdom you would like to impart into perpetuity? How about the famous, "I told you I was sick!" A friend of mine does not want to be cremated but her husband does—and he wants his ashes scattered. She wants her headstone to read, "Here Lies Mom. Dad's Around Somewhere."

Those words may not be *your* choice, but what would you like to say? This gravesite is where your family and friends will come periodically to be reminded of you, to feel close to you, and to feel your spirit. The words and artwork on the marker should convey a special meaning to those left behind.

LAST WORDS

In preplanning your final desires and wishes, it is important that you be an informed consumer.[13] Ask friends and clergy for recommendations for a reputable, long-in-the-community funeral home. Don't base your decisions solely on price, but on services provided.

Even if you have not made preplanned arrangements with a specific funeral home, if there are items pertinent to your obituary, your funeral, your burial arrangements that you want for your end-of-life arrangements, write everything down and make certain that your spouse knows where the papers are so they can be easily found when they are needed. Refer to the APPENDIX for information that your partner can find helpful. If you can gather all this material now and

---

[13] Retrieved 2 Feb 2013 from
www.cremationassociation.org/?page=WhatToAsk

have it readily on hand, it will save much time and energy during this particularly stressful time.

FINAL CLOSURE

Life goes on. The grieving process is real (see CHAPTER SIX). By preplanning your end-of-life issues, you have saved your surviving spouse from trying to make difficult decisions in the throes of debilitating unhappiness. You have also, hopefully, been able to satisfy the financial aspects of your choices. What a refreshing and long-remembered gift you have given to your loved one!

Action Items for This Chapter:

(1)   Write your own obituary.

(2)   Plan your funeral service.

(3)   Call or visit your favorite funeral home only for the purpose of getting information. Your funeral home has many forms to help trigger your memory for those specifics you need for your own pre-planning.

CHAPTER FIVE

THE MOST PRECIOUS GIFT
--or--THE GIVING OF CARE

⟨◠⟩

Never in the realms of my thoughts, when I said "I do," did I ever believe I would be a Caregiver (with a capital "C"). Who in their life says, "When I grow up I want to be a Caregiver"? Unless someone plans professionally to go that route (and bless their souls--- they are indeed angels of mercy), no-one even *thinks* of that possibility, much less probability.

I had been a giver-of-care before in my life. In raising children, I had patched "boo-boos" and wiped tears. I had cleaned up both ends after wicked cases of the flu. Gary and I (and our adult girls) had nursed Gary's elderly mother in her home for about six weeks before she died. That had included oxygen, hand-feeding, diapering, and very delicate bathing--but it hadn't lasted long.

So I was not a complete novice to the requirements of home health care--or so I thought. But never had I believed I would be taking care of a dying husband. It was certainly not the plan.

THIS ISN'T HAPPENING TO US

Both in our young 60s, we were counting the months when we could retire and spend the remainder of our healthy days traveling and enjoying our cabin. We were already loving being new grandparents.

94

We had almost finished the cabin; we had been building it for a little over five years. We were beginning to enjoy the fruits of hard labor when Gary got sick. That last summer at the cabin before Gary died was so painful.

Gary required full-time oxygen by now and did have a harder time breathing when we were at the higher altitude. He had always enjoyed puttering around when we were there, but now all he did was sit and look out the window. Even when I asked, he would not tell me what he was thinking. We both were still going along as though nothing was happening--well, except for the oxygen. But we never talked about it.

> *Sept 8/98 - Things are not going well--Gary is really struggling to do what little bit he does. I thought when we got to the lower altitude he would recover, but he hasn't. He said he was feeling better this morning when he got up . . . but was completely drained by the time I got home.*

When a person is dying, there are only a few choices—either put the patient in the hospital or a nursing home, or keep the family member at home to die. Until the 1960s, a sick person was taken to the hospital to receive tests and medical measures, supposedly to get better. If the doctor's diagnoses was that the person was dying, the patient was either sent home (which was very rare except in economic circumstances) or was kept in the hospital to die.

But dying persons were treated quite differently. They were most often transferred to a different wing of the hospital (not close to other patients who were recuperating) and, even though the actions were inadvertent and not deliberate, the caretaking was mostly detached and impersonal. Doctors and nurses had not been trained in end-of-life issues and were uncomfortable in caring for the dying--not understanding what to say or do.

Sedatives and pain killers were given--but not too many. After all, the doctors did not want the patient to become addicted! That wasn't the medical team's fault. They were under strict laws as to how many pain killers could be administered. (Thank goodness common sense eventually prevailed on that issue and dying patients are now given what they need to control their pain.)

The dying patient was still a human being with fears and questions about what was happening and what was going to happen, but neither he nor his family was necessarily included in the plans for his care. The family and friends had to abide by the hospital's rigid visiting hours and were only allowed to attend to their dear one at certain times of the day.

Caretaking for the dying person was archaic and frightening. Except for a periodic, sympathetic and understanding medical angel, the patient was mostly alone--left to his pain, fear and prayers.

Then, two miracles happened. Dr. Elisabeth Kubler-Ross, a psychiatrist, introduced the world to five particular stages that the dying person experiences: denial, anger, bargaining, depression and acceptance.[14] This ground-breaking theory served to change the prevailing attitudes toward the dying person and his or her voyage toward death.

Recognizing and allowing for these phases and attitudes permitted the medical teams treating the dying patients to be more understanding and compassionate. It gave them insight into emotions that they could recognize and identify, and with those pieces of information it helped them to not be so fearful of the dying process.

At the same time (1960s) Dame Cicely Saunders, a British physician, developed a new way of caring for those with a terminal prognosis. She proposed that a dying patient not be treated with the same type of care that was developed for curing a patient who was sick ("curative" care), which served only as an insult to the dying person and the person's deteriorating body.

Dr. Saunders proposed that the dying patient be treated in a peaceful surrounding, given "palliative" care to ease the sometimes painful and frightening symptoms, and helped to facilitate the journey from this life into whatever life the patient believed was to come next.

Dr. Saunders stated to her dying patients, "You matter because you are. You matter until the last moment of your life, and we will do all we can not only to help you die peacefully but also to help you live until you die."[15]

In 1967, St. Christopher's Hospice was opened by Dr. Saunders in London. And between Dr. Kubler-Ross and Dr. Saunders, an entirely new way of looking at death was developed.

---

[14] Retrieved 2 Feb 2013 from en.wikipedia.org/wiki/Elisabeth Kubler Ross
[15] Dame Cicely Saunders, quoted in <u>Final Gifts</u> by Maggie Callanan and Patricia Kelley (New York: Bantam Books reissue 2008) p 25

Between the entirely new motivations and outlooks of these two incredibly far-reaching women, the Hospice movement was begun.

Fifty years later, Hospice has grown and expanded and is considered to be the qualitative movement in assisting the dying person through the end-of life process. In that fifty years, however, Dr. Kubler-Ross's hypothesis has undergone critical analysis and scrutiny as further research has proven that not every dying person experiences all five of the responses or in any particular order.

Dr. Kubler-Ross agreed at the end of her life that the "stages" were never meant to be compartmentalized into neat, sequential packages. But her efforts in establishing the theories still helped the medical profession to see that the dying person was an individual with feelings and basic emotions that needed to be met, and respected, to the very end of life.[16]

Upon reading the journal entries I made the year before Gary's death, I recognized the emotions that Dr. Kubler-Ross had identified—and a few more. And they came like waves—never solid, always moving backward and forward with the ebb and tide, sometimes crashing, sometimes placidly rolling over the top of each other. The emotions were valid, whether her rigid theories were, or not.

THIS CAN'T BE HAPPENING TO US!

When things were beginning to look grim and Gary finally began to admit the reality of what was happening to him, we could no longer deny the certainty of the future. And we both were becoming extremely angry. It was a horrible time and I have to admit that I did not help the situation. What I did not understand at the time was that, even though I was not the one who was dying, I was experiencing the same emotions. Anger and loss was ravaging both of us.

If there was a yeller in the family it was certainly I. As a normally placid person, it took a great deal to get Gary riled up. I was not accustomed to his yelling at me and being, generally, angry with me and what I was doing--or not doing.

---

[16] Ruth Davis Konigsberg. "New Ways to Think About Grief" Time Magazine 29 January 2011

I knew nothing except how to argue back and defend myself. I did not stop to realize or understand that he was angry because of what he was losing--and I was the one he took it out on. Each task he could no longer perform, each responsibility he could no longer meet, was a loss to him. He was not only losing his functional capacity, he was losing his identity--and he was grieving those losses. He was lashing out, and I was in the crosshairs.

> *Sept 20/98 - Many times I have given in just to save a fight . . . I'm ordering a pizza . . . and he's yelling at me that I'm doing it wrong. I put my hand over the mouth piece and literally yelled at him to SHUT UP! I don't think I've said that to anyone since I was a child---and how embarrassing and childish it was. After I hung up I yelled at him that if I'm going to be responsible for doing something, he has to let me do it! I am so wearing down . . . I told Cathy [neighbor] yesterday that it's probably a good thing I've been such a S.O.B. all my life so that I'm tough enough to do all this. Maybe I was wrong--I certainly don't seem to be very tough!*

Authors Maggie Callanan and Patricia Kelley, in their book *Final Gifts*, say the anger and frustration "can stem from helplessness at losing control and becoming dependent on others." These two hospice nurses say that the anger and helplessness is most often directed at the safest place—to those who are the closest, usually family and friends. "In the presence of such vehemence, it's very hard to avoid feeling hurt. Responding sharply often leads to arguments which rarely accomplish anything."[17]

We continued to fight. Even now I feel guilty, knowing it was not me he was angry with, but it was the disease. I went in there with my dukes up, ready to defend myself, when I should have been smarter and recognized what was really happening.

After some gut-wrenching, soul-searching communication, and after we recognized and conceded to each other what we were doing, we apologized profusely and literally moved on. That mostly ended a horrible segment of our journey—one that I only wish had not happened.

The stress was getting to me, still I had no idea what was lying in wait as Gary got progressively worse. We never talked about it.

---

[17] Maggie Callanan and Patricia Kelley. Final Gifts (New York: Bantam Books, reissue 2008) p 42

From the day we learned his condition was terminal, it was simply the assumption that he would stay at home and I would care for him-- through to the end. With no knowledge as to what was expected of me and no training in what was going to happen, I jumped in, trying to exude confidence--more for myself than for Gary.

Does one ever know how to take care of a terminally ill patient? I certainly did not and was working only on my own intuitions. At the time there were no classes or instruction. Now on the web there are hundreds of places to go for help. But remember, this was in the late 90s when, for me, a web was mostly associated with spiders. I was on my own and my own gut instincts.

Caring for someone with a terminal illness is a very frightening prospect. Different patients have different symptoms, and for the layperson to think of caring for another in the face of nausea, vomiting, diarrhea, incontinence, constipation, bed sores, weight loss, dementia, kidney dialysis, feeding tubes, and a variety of other ailments and procedures, is overwhelming. Dispensing pills is one thing, but giving shots, drawing blood and checking vital signs and statistics is another.

In addition to the day-to-day obligations, caregiving of a spouse can also involve dealing with all of the legal and medical documents, including those regarding end-of-life realities. Decisions for medical care should be agreed upon with the physicians, and procedures for care taught to the caretaking spouse. The home may have to be modified to accommodate the patient's needs, even to the point of structural remodeling. Distraught family members may object to and intrude on the caretaker's chosen methods of care. In the depths of the emotional roller-coaster rides, the caretaker/spouse's heart and mind can be stretched beyond limitations.

The caretaker's capacity to continue, day and night, night and day, is compromised by the resentment and guilt--and loneliness-- that can fester if left unchecked. Many times, all the caretaker needs to know is that he or she has the support of family and friends--and is appreciated! Simple gestures, such as a "thank you," or, "let me take over and you can have the afternoon off," can be of paramount importance in being able to carry on with this never-ending task.

All difficulties aside, research shows that the nursing given by family and friends is most often the best possible. This is the nurturing that maintains the patient's comfort and dignity to the end. It is the caretaking filled with personal love—a most precious gift.

Gary's and my situation was not unusual—in fact, we were pretty typical. According to the *Family Caregiver Alliance 2011*, more than one in ten workers is involved in caretaking. This means that there are currently more than 66 million Americans engaged in unpaid caregiving for the ill, the disabled and/or the elderly.

In a report conducted by the National Alliance for Caregiving (NAC) in collaboration with AARP, and funded by the MetLife Foundation, the statistic was reported that, despite the stereotype that the majority of caregivers are women, one third of the American caregivers are men.[18]

Author Gail Sheehy reported in 2010 that, even though the NAC study indicated that one-third of the caregivers are men, it was also discovered that most of the men are doing administrative type tasks and are only half as likely to assist in the most personal caretaking such as bathing, diapering or toileting the patient. Sheehy says that the men she interviewed told her, "It isn't seen as manly."[19] That is not to say, however, that there are not those brave, sensitive, unusual husbands who will take on the intimate, daily care of their wives. Kudos and hurrahs to them!

What makes a family decide to care for the ill relative at home? The reasons are vast and varied, but it's mostly the love and concern for the dying person that supersedes any other anticipated personal discomfort. The one and main goal is to maintain the dignity and worth of the patient throughout an experience that could so easily take all of that away in a cold (or luke-warm) professional setting. Another reason is the cost of outside professional care which can be astronomical and beyond the reach of the average family. Often it is the default position to keep Uncle Harry at home with Aunt Millie doing the caretaking. And many times, Aunt Millie is in need of a caretaker, herself. Many caregivers of older people are themselves older, and many of them are in fair to poor health.

Remember that you *must not* be ashamed if you cannot—for whatever reason—take on the burdens of caretaking in your home! Making that decision depends on the caretaker's age and health, the

---

[18] Retrieved 15 Feb 2013 from National Alliance for Caregiving/AARP National Caregiver Survey 2003
[19] Gail Sheehy, "The Secret Caregivers" AARP Magazine May 2010

patient's degree of illness, the support (both physical, emotional and financial) that will be there for both the caretaker and the patient, and many other decisions personal to only you. Sometimes, even though the love and the desire is there, the possibility is not.

Well, I dug in, reading what I could, listening to the wisdom of others, and mostly going by the seat of my pants. I do readily recognize now that my caregiving was pretty minimal in relation to what some caregivers give. Gary was sick for months (sick for years, but *really* sick for just months).

Many caregivers are bound to their duties for years and years. And Gary was not addled or challenged with dementia. He was lucid and coherent almost to the end. Many home caregivers are left to deal with their patient's confusion, rage, unrealistic demands or negative thoughts and reasoning. For them, the upheaval goes on for years.

In September Gary was not yet bedridden. He was still driving a little bit, but found getting around hard to manage after he was out of the car. The unbidden elephant in the living room was growing larger and larger and turning many shades of bright pink. We talked about what was happening as we tried to solve immediate problems. But the end seemed so far away, and we still didn't talk about what was going to happen..

Sept 28/98 - We hit a milestone--we got a wheelchair. I needed the "lightweight" so I can lift it in and out of the car. It still weighs a heck of a lot! Gary is not doing well. Sometimes he sits and sits on the edge of the bed, all hunched over with such a vacant look. He's angry, sometimes ornery, and downright rude sometimes.

Oct 1/98 - The maiden voyage of the wheelchair was not too successful-- but I learned a lot for the next time. I think I learned how to unfold it and fold it back. But I will practice before the next time. I think Gary had a good time--he was most proud that he had "made it." The other thing I need to figure out is how to get through doors, and how to negotiate bumps (others were helpful and we did make it).

Oct 6/98 - I talked with Gary's doctor for about 15-20 minutes. He said he could give Gary a "patch" with a narcotic to help ease his frantic breathing. I remember last spring when he said he would give him that at the end! . . . We can't be at the end! . . . He still showers himself and shaves himself--though not every day. And it gets harder and harder. But we can't be near the end--we just can't be . . .

101

Oct 12/98 - They delivered liquid oxygen today. He's been on a very noisy condenser that no longer gives him a high enough dose. He says he's feeling much better at the higher dose when he has to get around. He has been treating me very very well! I guess our blow up was part of all this. Too bad something so awful was so necessary.

Oct 19/98 - The liquid oxygen has helped immensely! Also, the doctor prescribed a narcotic patch which administers a slow steady dose of narcotic. It has made a significant difference . . . The patch does seem to have helped him not breathe quite as rapidly as he does upon any exertion . . . We went to the clinic and got our flu shots today. I wheeled Gary in the wheelchair. He was so garrulous he was almost to the point of being giddy. He was happily gabbing with everyone around.

Gary and I learned the hard way that, whenever he went to see the doctor, I needed to go along also. Even when I did go, each of us would hear something different and end up disagreeing over what had been said and what we had been told to do. We learned to take a note book and write down what the doctor said. Better yet (which we didn't do), take a tape recorder to record the information the doctor is giving you--as well as the directions you need to follow. You can then play the recording for others in the family so they can be fully aware of the situation. We could have saved many misunderstandings between ourselves and among our kids if we had done that.

Oct 25/98 - Gary told me today that his goal is to see the year 2000! Wow!

ADVANCE DIRECTIVE, aka LIVING-WILL

Gary's long-time friend, an estate attorney, had met with us earlier in the month and had completed our estate planning (see CHAPTER TWO) getting our legal papers finalized and ultimately saving us quite a bit of money in estate taxes (the cap was much lower then). He also drafted a living will for us and also a form for a health-care proxy.

What is a living will? A living will is *not* the same thing as a will! A will designates how your assets are to be passed on to your heirs.

A living will also is *not* the same thing as a living trust! A living trust, also, designates how your assets are to be passed on. (Oh, it's all so confusing!)

A living will is an Advance Directive--directions that you give to others, in advance, that convey your decisions about your end-of-life care. Sometimes the Advance Directive is confused with a DNR, or a Do Not Resuscitate, but in some cases, they can be one and the same thing. The DNR is more particularly used to notify the paramedics who have been called (to save your life) that you do not want herculean measures performed on you. If your desire is that you absolutely do not want them to resuscitate you if you have stopped breathing, you need to sign a Do Not Resuscitate form and leave it where the paramedics or other immediate responders can find it. If they cannot visibly see it (e.g., taped to your headboard, on the refrigerator, etc.), or if no-one is there to give it to them, they are bound by their professional ethics to do everything they can to save you, which includes resuscitation.

The Advance Directive is more comprehensive and gives directions beyond resuscitation. If you are no longer able to communicate, this document directs others as to what kind of medical care you want. Many questions need to be addressed in this directive: if you know that your condition is terminal, how much medical care do you wish to have? Do you want to have medical care that can extend your life for days or months? Do you want an all-out effort to save you, or would you prefer to be kept comfortable with no pain, and be allowed to die peacefully?

You can choose to accept or refuse medical care. Do you want to be resuscitated if your breathing or your heartbeat stops? Do you want to be hooked up to life-sustaining machines in the hopes that you can recover? Do you want to have tube feeding if you can no longer eat? What about water and/or antibiotics? Do you wish to donate your tissues or organs?

More questions for you to consider:

- If you have been diagnosed with a terminal illness that also brings a great amount of pain, would you want to be sedated to the point of being unconscious? Or, would you rather push through the pain so that in your last days you are lucid and coherent?

- Which do you fear most about end-of-life happenings?
  - being in pain.
  - loss of control - not being able to think clearly and make choices for yourself.
  - being a physical, emotional and financial burden on your loved ones.
  - something else personal only to you.
- If you are terminally ill and you get pneumonia, do you want aggressive antibiotic treatment or palliative (comfort) care?
- Are there circumstances that you would consider worse than death?
- Where do you want (or not want) to receive care? (home, nursing facility, hospital?)
- Do you have special religious beliefs that would guide your end-of-life decisions?

Some states have enacted laws that allow a Physician Order for Life-Sustaining Treatment, or POLST. This is similar to an Advance Directive with a few differences. A POLST becomes effective the *moment it is signed* and is not contingent on future changes in the patient's condition (as is the Advance Directive). It does not require the Health Care Proxy.

This is not a do-it-yourself form. In order to be valid, it must be prepared by a licensed medical person and should be used to document your preferences when you are a patient. Some states have not advanced the POLST in their laws, but your health-care provider will know whether a POLST is allowed in your specific state.

Creating an Advance Directive (or a POLST) helps you face the unavoidable end-of-life situation that comes to us all. It helps you come to grips with your personal philosophy about dying.

Everyone wants to have a "good death," but that might mean different things for different people. Now is the time to examine-- deeply--your core values and how they will play in your end-of-life decisions. Spiritual beliefs will usually play a large part in what you decide.

Think carefully about the ramifications of your decisions for yourself and others and what long-lasting effect(s) they might have.

REVERSING AN ADVANCE DIRECTIVE or a POLST

To change or revoke your Advance Directive, you may destroy it or write "revoked" across the old one. You can then get your attorney to help you write a new one. Be certain that a competent adult witness knows what you are doing and preferably signs and dates a statement to that end. If other copies of your directive have been given to other people, gather those back in, or at least, notify everyone that you are making changes and ask them to destroy whatever forms you may have given them.

Give a copy of the updated directive to your primary care doctor and make certain he or she understands your wishes and will be supportive of you and what you want. When entering a hospital or nursing home, ensure that a copy of your directive is placed in your medical files. Know where to find the form quickly in case of an emergency.

Inform your Health Care Proxy (see next section) of the new directive and make certain he or she has a copy or knows where to hurriedly find it. By giving copies to other family members they, at least, know your wishes, and hopefully will be supportive of you and not question your end-of-life requests.

To void a POLST, the patient may *orally* inform emergency service personnel or any other adult witness of the wish to revoke the order, may write "void" across or may destroy the form, or may ask another adult to void or destroy the form. It is significantly easier to void a POLST than an Advance Directive.

HEALTH CARE PROXY

When you are in the hospital, hopefully you will be able to speak for yourself. If so, the doctors will listen to you. Your word will supersede anything you may have signed on your Advance Directive or on your POLST.

But if you *cannot* speak for yourself, there needs to be someone who can represent you and can speak on your behalf. Even though you would assume so, sometimes the Advance Directive alone does not ensure that your wishes will be met. Physicians are sometimes unwilling to follow the directives of a living will when it concerns ending life-sustaining measures.

Envision yourself in the hospital where there is a medical team that is not willing to follow your written directive of no life-sustaining measures, including artificial respiration. Also envision a person in the room whom: (1) you have chosen to speak on your behalf, (2) you have told this person—both orally and in writing--exactly what your wishes are, and (3) you have given him or her a copy of your Advance Directive. In addition, this person has a written Power of Attorney for Health Care from you giving him or her permission to act on your behalf.

Even with all this documentation, I can attest from personal experience that the medical team will still be cautiously hesitant to withdraw life sustaining support. But they--*by law*--will eventually be required to accede to your wishes.

How do you choose your proxy? Do not choose a person who is not close to you and who would not assiduously look after your best interests. This is a time when you are vulnerable and when it would be easy for someone to take advantage of you.

You need to choose a person whom you have known for a considerable length of time and in whom you have explicit trust. You need to have the belief and comfort that this person will look after your interests *in spite of what his or her personal interests*, for your care, might be. And let everyone know whom you have chosen to represent you.

Choose someone who can be a strong advocate for you when dealing with unresponsive medical staff. Choose someone who has the respect and support of your family members and who is not afraid to talk honestly with you about sensitive issues. It is probably best to designate a person who is younger than you (okay---so they'll still be around when you need them). You need an advocate who can stay strong in an extremely stressful situation and cannot be bowed by other, however well-meaning, persons.

When you *ask* someone to be your proxy, explain clearly what you expect. Share your end-of-life philosophies. Don't assume he or she will agree to serve as your proxy. You need to know that whoever you choose will be there when needed! The proxy needs to be able to act "as" you, not necessarily "for" you.

Do not choose a representative from the staff of the assisted living facility where you live, or from your doctor's office, or from your book club. Do not pick someone you do not intimately know.

106

Deal cautiously when choosing your spouse to be your advocate. Sometimes a spouse is too close and cannot be objective when the time comes. Or—sometimes, a spouse is *exactly* the person you want to be there for you.

Your state might have specific state-approved forms (for both the Advance Directive and the Health Care Proxy) that need to be completed and signed in order to be valid documents. The legal document identifying your proxy (your advocate) is called a "Durable Power of Attorney for Healthcare." This may have a different name in your state, but it should include the terms "power of attorney" and "for healthcare." You should be able to find these forms on your state's web site. It's also advisable to contact an attorney in your state to make certain the forms are valid and meet the specific state's requirements.

ORGAN DONATION

Family members can sometimes get very unreasonable over your choices of end-of-life issues--particularly that of organ donation. Donating organs can mean different things to different people depending on their level of understanding of what organ donation is.

Almost everyone knows of heart and liver transplants, but fewer people understand that tissues can be donated, such as skin, bone marrow, heart valves, corneas, and much more. A possible complicating factor that you may face is that organs must receive blood until they are removed from the body, so it may be necessary to temporarily place you, the donor, on a breathing machine--*even if that goes against your directive.*

If organ donation is your choice, have you completed an organ donor card that is easily located? Have you registered as an organ donor and is it reflected on your driver's license? An organ donor card is similar to an Advance Directive--it serves to inform others of your decision. But it can also serve to comfort remaining dear ones who are uneasy with this thought and who might try to undo your decision. Your proxy can be of benefit at this time in defending your choices and in helping to pacify those who would disagree with you.

If your body is too old, however, the organs have already done their thing (of keeping you alive) and may be worn out and not

107

suitable for transplant. In that case you can choose to donate your entire body to a medical school for study (believe it or not---they will even take old, used-up bodies). If you feel that is too radical, you can agree to have an autopsy done and used for study purposes.

The body of an organ donor can still be shown in a coffin and there will be no outward signs of the donations having been made or of there having been an autopsy.

MEDICAL AND FINANCIAL SUPPORT

Nov 16/98 - Can't believe a whole week has gone by. I've been quite sick. Have gone to work, but felt awful. Last Friday I was talking to Ted [my boss] about taking Family Medical Leave. I am so exhausted! I don't see how I can continue this pace.

Things were getting worse. I was trying to decide what to do about working--how to juggle the combination of sick leave and vacation leave I had accumulated over the years. I knew I would need to use those hours at some time in the future, so I was hesitant to use the sick leave for myself even though I was quite sick.

When the male is the caregiver, he usually continues to work and either hires caregivers during the day or finds a volunteer from family or friends to fill in while he is at work.

When the female is the caregiver and she is trying to continue to work, it is considerably more difficult. She usually has a lower paying job, probably with no or few benefits. She may have to give up her job in order to do the caretaking.

The Family and Medical Leave Act is a federal law that grants you, the caretaker, up to twelve unpaid weeks of time off with a guarantee of a job when you are ready to return. In some cases twelve weeks will be enough. But in most cases, especially in cases of Alzheimer's or dementia, twelve weeks is just the beginning.

There is a program of Home Health Services that is paid for by Medicare, but these services are for short-term, intermediate, skilled care at home, for someone who is expected to get better.

There is NO HELP from Medicare for long-term, unskilled care. Persons with severe and chronic illnesses or disabilities, whether being taken care of at home or in a professional facility, can expect to get no help from Medicare or from most health insurance plans. Long-term care is extremely expensive and can easily expend the limit of a person's financial resources.

If the patient has been thinking of the future and has purchased an insurance policy of Long-Term Care, now is the time to benefit from that planning. Each policy is different and has different coverage, but the infusion of financial help can be invaluable at this time. But even this type policy has financial limits.

There is a joint federal and state program, Medicaid, which helps pay most costs for long-term care provided your income and resources are limited. Medicaid covers health care costs, prescription drugs, and nursing-home care (in a Medicaid-certified facility). Medicaid coverage varies from state to state depending on what the state programs entail. But in order to qualify for Medicaid, a person's assets have to be depleted to almost nothing. This can present major complications for the spouse who is left behind.

There is a little known federal program available for veterans and veteran's spouses called the Veterans Aid and Attendance benefit provided by the Department of Veterans Affairs. The program provides assistance to vets and/or their spouses when they can no longer live on their own and are in an assisted living or nursing home facility. The program is based on need but, unlike Medicaid, the person's assets don't have to be completely drained.[20]

Hospice, which will be discussed in more detail later in this chapter, is covered 100% by Medicare, but the patient has to be diagnosed as terminally ill with, provided the illness runs it's normal course, a six-month prognosis.

There are state programs that can help, but few people ever learn about what is available until there is a major crisis (or sometimes after). You need to know where to look and/or whom to ask. The Internet is a great resource for finding local and/or state programs.

If you live in a small community with few resources you can access the state-wide opportunities and go from there. Most are financially limited, but they can still give you some assistance. Keep asking until you get the help you need. Become a nuisance, if that's what it takes.[21]

---

[20] "Veteran's Aid and Attendance" retrieved 4 April 2013
www.seniorcareassociates.com

[21] Retrieved 2 February 2013 from www.medicare.gov/caregivers/paying for care

Nov 28/98 - Gary is getting so weak I wonder how he keeps going.....He works every day on a schedule of things he has to do. I wonder why.

Nov 29/98 - We went to church – it took all he had. Thank goodness for the wheelchair. He told me tonight he really thinks he'll make it to 2000. He said he's been particularly close to the Lord lately, and he knows he will live to finish his work – letters to the kids and grandkids, his personal history and that of his dad's. I pray only that I can continue to do what I need to do.

By now the back bedroom had been turned into the equivalent of a military hospital room. There is no information on how to set up an efficient sick room where everything is at hand and yet not being tripped over. The room was already snug with the queen-size bed, a dresser and a chest of drawers. And Gary was a ham radio operator, so we had a large credenza-type desk in the room with book shelves and drawers which held his radio equipment. In the middle of the room was a smaller desk with his computer, a separate keyboard and a printer.

Add to this a desk chair, a walker, two canes, two forms of oxygen (one, a large condenser), a potty chair, a urinal, a wheelchair, a cooler with immediate snacks in it, and bottles and bottles of half-used medicines. A gallon-size jug of water with a spout was on the desk so he could easily get a drink of water when I was not immediately available.

Medicines were hard to keep track of. Gary wanted to be in control of his medicines, but I began counting the pills in the bottles so I would know exactly what he was taking and not taking. When I explained to him that he was not taking his prescriptions accurately, he reluctantly agreed to let me make a chart of what he was taking and when.

I finally had to put the medicines where he could not find them, because he couldn't remember what he'd taken (or not) and he would forget to tally what he had taken on the chart. I hated taking that piece of independence away from him, but I felt I must. In retrospect—did it matter? He was dying anyway. Did it matter what he was taking?

Whether he noticed or not, he never said anything, I tried to make certain that there were always fresh flowers on the dresser.

Once in a while balloons were brought in. My hope was that it would brighten the ominous ambience of the room.

Gary would sit at his ham radio for hours and talk or monitor the radio calls. He talked a lot with a close friend in Tennessee and with other friends who were local. And he dictated his history as he was lying in bed into an old dictating machine I had brought home from work.

> *Dec 2/98 - Gary .. talked today of living 2-3 more years. I called Hospice of Utah yesterday to ask for help in getting him showered – it is such a <u>chore</u> for him. And yet when I told him, he flatly refused saying he can do it and he <u>wants</u> to keep doing it and he doesn't need help. I wonder if he knows how sick he is. And if he does, how does he keep fighting. And then I think maybe he doesn't think he is so sick, and so he just stays positive and "up." I wonder about myself and how I can be so analytical about what is happening. Sometimes I feel like I'm on the outside recording this tragedy and that it's not really my long-time companion who will very soon not be around. I don't allow myself to dwell on that. I feel I must stay up for him and not let him see me sad, because then I'm telling him you're going to die and I'm sad.*
>
> *. . . It would be so much better if we could talk about the end, but when I even intimate it could be sooner than later, he won't hear it. I can only deal with it all by turning off my emotions.*

All day long Gary would make lists and agendas of things he needed to do. Gary was CERT trained (Crisis Emergency Response Team) and, in context with that certification, he had previously taught classes on how to become licensed as a ham radio operator. Many months prior, he had promised to teach one of those classes in our neighborhood. Organizing this class and being able to shower by himself seemed to be the only two objectives that gave his life some purpose. And he was tenaciously hanging onto both of them. (After he was gone I found notebook after notebook with lists and lists of items needing to be covered for the radio class. He was not going to miss anything!)

> *Dec 5/98 - Gary is so weak . . . He can only walk 5-10 feet now before he needs to sit down. In his room he transfers from his bed to his chair. He talks a fair amount on his radio and does a little computer work. He is*

111

actually organizing a ham radio class for our church to start in January. He was . . . asked last summer [by one of the church leaders] *to do this. I guess he figures he better get going.*

Dec 6/98 - I had a really long talk with Renee [my sister] *this afternoon . . . I asked her if she thought Steve* [my brother-in-law] *could come once a week and give Gary a shower. She thought Steve would love to do that. I told Gary later tonight and he jumped all over me. He said, "Will you get off worrying about my shower?" He was breathless and said he'd talk later. After he was in bed he called me in and apologized. He said that being able to shower himself is very private, and he'd like to do it by himself as long as possible. He also said that not being able to do it is a milestone <u>down</u> for him and that's another reason he wanted to do it as long as he can. He thanked me for all I do and said he appreciated what I had said . . . yesterday in church . . . when I said he was showing all of us courage and how to be valiant, and how much I love and admire him. I truly meant it.*

KEEP YOUR "I LOVE YOUs" UP-TO-DATE

Since Gary died I have given a lot of thought to whether it's worse for a surviving spouse to experience the immediate, unexpected death of his or her partner, or whether it's worse to watch a spouse languish and deteriorate before dying. I will say this: as difficult as it was to live through the day-by-day horrors of watching Gary's decline and as long as it took, there was an outstanding positive. We had the opportunity, over and over, to apologize to each other for the failures and unhappy times we had brought to our marriage, and we had the chance to ask the other for forgiveness—which we both freely gave (and received). We told each other on a daily basis how much we loved each other. We hadn't done that in a long, long time. And Gary died having had all those issues resolved and forgiven. And my issues had been resolved and forgiven, as well.

The need for reconciliation is of paramount importance--for both parties. As a person is dying, it's impossible not to think of the old grievances--the old hurts and bad feelings. What an opportunity it would be, in order to die in peace, to be able to reconcile those matters that have been left undone by apologizing to and asking for forgiveness, or better yet, by expressing gratitude to someone who has made a particular, life-affirming difference.

What happens when there is a sudden death of a spouse and those reconciliations haven't happened? My advice is this: keep your "I love you's" up to date. Take care of those unresolved issues that bring angst to your marriage. Remember to sincerely tell each other "I love you" on a regular basis. After your spouse is gone, don't carry guilt for unsettled matters that you will never again have the chance to get resolved.

Gary and I had the opportunity to take care of all of that, and my mind is at ease. One never knows what will happen at any time. Say what needs to be said--then rest easy.

Dec 29/98 - I called the doctor today because Gary thinks he has a cold. The doc told me about hospice and what they could do for us. He said they only deal with patients who are terminal within six months. I asked him if we were there, and he said, yes. He said they'll come to our home and assess where we are--for physical and emotional needs. Gary agreed it would be a good idea. He has not been feeling well at all. I don't know if it's the cold he says he has, or if he's starting to give up . . .

Jan 4/99 - . . . This disease is so agonizingly slow. It just nips away micrometers at a time. I know now when I told different doctors two to three years ago that my husband had IPF, why they winced and said how sorry they were. I had no idea it would be so tedious – that it would entail such a horrible slow-motion wasting away.

Gary was so sick I was quite surprised how angry he got with the doctor whom he had previously liked and respected. I suppose it was suddenly being told that he was *not* going to live to the year 2000. Gary felt as though the doctor was abandoning him--over to hospice--and he told him so. He did not appreciate being left at a time like this. I don't know if he thought if he got mad at the doctor that the doctor could change things? It was so unlike Gary and was most unsettling.

Jan 7/99 - Hospice came today . . . a young nurse who was very compassionate, but straightforward. She explained that hospice comes in when the doctor indicates the patient has six months or less to live. Gary was brought up short with that information because I had not told him about that before. He was very upset and said he felt that our doctor had cut him off and wasn't interested in treating him anymore. I told him that wasn't true, but I could tell he wasn't sure about that. The nurse explained all our options – that if we go on hospice that we need to understand that herculean measures are not done. In other words, if there's a crisis, we call hospice and not 911, because 911 has to do all they can to prolong life . . . Hospice can then come and ease the patient with medication – ultimately to their death (my words, not theirs). Gary was pretty somber after she left . . . About 5:15 the doctor called US! He talked to both of us for about ½ hour! I don't know if the hospice nurse told him about Gary's reaction that he thought the doctor was cutting him off, but he kept reassuring Gary that he was there for him for whatever. Gary was very brusque and still angry. The doctor answered all the questions we had. He said hospice was one of our options, but certainly not mandatory. Then Gary asked him about the six months--and he hedged. He back pedaled and said, well, we certainly don't know, etc. etc. I guess that was okay. Gary has had the seed planted, and we can only go from there.

HOSPICE

Any patient who has been diagnosed with a terminal illness and who has a prognosis of six months or less, provided the disease is to run its normal course, is eligible for Hospice. (It should be noted here that if the patient lives beyond six months, the patient will not be discontinued in the Hospice program. Hospice will be there as long as the patient needs them.) Hospice, considered as the most recognizable and reputable care offered at the end of a person's life, is a philosophy and an approach of helping someone to live with comfort, dignity and well-being--to the end. Hospice is about helping the patient to "live well" the days that are remaining. They are there to answer the patient's needs--physical, psychological or spiritual. Hospice is covered 100% by Medicare

Hospice also focuses on the emotional and spiritual well-being of the family. It consists of a team that includes the attending physician, the hospice physician, nurses, hospice health-care aides, trained volunteers, spiritual counselors, social workers and anyone and anything else the patient might need. There is someone on-call 24/7—around the clock—to provide comfort meds and equipment. Hospice nurses coach the families on what to expect at the end so the symptoms will not seem so frightening.

The most unsettling aspect of using and relying on the Hospice team is that the caretaker and/or family must agree *not* to call 911 for emergency life-saving procedures. It's hard, when involved in the extreme and frightening suffering of the patient, not to be caught up in the desire to be saved or for your dear one to be saved. Hospice should be called first and they will respond immediately with palliative, comforting, pain-relieving care.

One of the reasons doctors are hesitant to refer their patients to hospice is, first of all, they hate to admit defeat and think they have failed. They try to keep all hope alive, not only with the families, but with themselves, as well. A second reason is that many times the doctors don't really know when a patient is going to die---maybe it's within six months, maybe it's longer.

Jan 9/99 - Gary is resisting using hospice. I suppose I don't blame him.

The ham radio class began, but he was too ill and couldn't be there to start it. I went over to the class to represent him. The instructor (Gary had lined up all the weekly instructors for the eight weeks of the class) called Gary on the radio. Gary welcomed the students, gave them an introduction to the class—all from his bedroom. He had completed his goal of creating the radio class.

But what incentive does a dying person have to eat? The physical changes to a dying person's body are profound and upsetting. And when they don't eat, they become weaker and less able to get around--even from the bed to the bathroom.

Jan 16/99 - Gary let me help shower him . . . It's the first time I've see him nude for a long time, and as he walked away from me my heart broke as I saw how skinny he is . . . his skin hangs on his bones . . .Even with me helping, it took about 1½ hours from start to finish.

DEPRESSION

PATIENT DEPRESSION

As the illness proceeds, many times the patient becomes isolated (within him or herself) and withdrawn. Where there was denial and anger over the losses, now there is depression. Sadness--and fear--becomes all encompassing, and the patient becomes more remote. The fear is not so much precipitated by the dying process, but from what it is going to take to get there. The fear and anxiety of possible pain and suffering at the end is depressing and debilitative.

The downhill slide is especially concerning and frightening to those who are around.

The patient can come to believe that others have given up. However, and usually slowly, when the stage of acceptance of the inevitable does come, the communication can open as the patient realizes there is still much to be said and talked about. Sometimes all the patient needs is to know that there is someone there to talk with.

Toward the very end, sometimes the patient's words don't make any sense and communication becomes difficult. By understanding and recognizing the signals of the dying process, the caretaker can help ease the burden by just listening and responding in the most appropriate way possible. The patient mostly needs to know that he or she is not alone.

CAREGIVER DEPRESSION

Many caregivers, especially those who minister sometimes for decades to the needs of another person (especially if the patient suffers from some form of dementia) are susceptible to serious depression and other health related issues. It's not only the feeding, the bathing, the medications, the taking care of the personal (and sometimes, embarrassing) needs of the patient, it's the laundry, the bill paying, the grocery shopping, the cooking, the cleaning, the family--all the regular day-to-day-responsibilities that need to be seen to. The commitments that were made to your spouse--and yourself--at the beginning of the illness are now overwhelming and becoming harder to live up to.

And if the superhuman efforts of the caregiver go unrecognized by others, but especially by the patient, the strength of the caregiver can easily waver. Burn-out can occur and depression follows.

Sometimes the depression becomes so all-encompassing the caregiver has nothing left to fight with and becomes overly exhausted and seriously ill. When the caregiving goes on day-in and day-out with no respite, it's natural for the caregiver to spiral down--emotionally and physically—easily reaching what is termed "rock bottom."

Sometimes it takes reaching that very bottom to discover the depths within ourselves. "If we let ourselves go all the way in and touch bottom, something magical happens," says Beth McLeod in *Caregiving*. "Just as becoming a caregiver has entailed taking a path

116

that reversed the direction of our life, so does another path open up at a certain stage of growth. At the summit of crisis, inner powers appear. A voice beckons, and it is time to leave the old life."[22]

When my daughter Valerie's baby boy was born severely premature and it was determined he would need to be taken care of for the rest of his life, Valerie pleaded with me, "What am I going to do? I can't do this!" My response was, "You can do this because you have no other choice." Three years later, I was making the same plea and she said the same thing to me, "You can do this because you have no other choice."

It is at this lowest place in our lives that we can hopefully uncover a strength not known before. It is at this point that our fear to what lies before us can open a doorway to walk through. McLeod says, "This juncture between past and future frames the remainder of the caregiving experience – and the rest of life."[23]

Feb 16/99 - It's starting to get really hard.....folks offer to help – but what can anyone do?

Sources exist to help us regain our strength. Take regular and planned breaks. Take time to enjoy a favorite activity with favorite people. Above all, get out of the house.

If at all possible, enjoy a pleasant interest with your spouse— maybe something as simple as reading to each other and discussing issues other than illnesses.

Good friends and family truly do want to help, but they don't know what to do. So they make a generic offer to help, then they walk away.

As the caretaker, sometimes it is easy to think you are the only one who knows what to do and how to care for your patient. Get over this idea immediately! For your own sanity, be humble enough (yes, humble) to accept help now and again.

Be ready for that question when someone says, "What can I do to help?" Have a list of items written on a notepad and ready to hand out. Rip off two or three and give to your prospective helper. Even a little help goes a long way and can make a big difference in

[22] Beth Witrogen McLeod, <u>Caregiving, the Spiritual Journey of Love, Loss, and Renewal</u> (New York: John Wiley & Sons, Inc. 1999) p 136
[23] McLeod, p 136

how you are feeling about yourself and your tasks. Give up thinking that you know best, and you might become open to new ideas and new ways of doing things.

Wanting a break, wanting some respite time away from the situation, is not a sign of weakness, nor is it a sign that you are not willing, nor can no longer continue to provide the 100% day-in and day-out care for your partner. There are many studies that identify respite as the most needed service for caregivers.

When you are traveling, do you remember the directions from the flight attendants to first put the oxygen mask on yourself before assisting those who need help? This is a perfect example of the importance of taking care of yourself first so that you will be better able to take care of others.

Ask hospice for help. Don't wait until you are desperate--get the help while you are still in pretty good shape. Getting that assistance early on will help you stay in better shape for a longer period of time.

Hospice can provide a social worker to answer some of your questions, spiritual support to give you that extra needed boost, volunteers who can sit with the patient so that you can be free to do whatever your pleasure dictates for a couple of times a week. Hospice is there to provide that respite-type of resource.

> *Feb 11/99 - I had an appointment for lunch today with one of my instructors. I just didn't feel I had it in me to expend any energy making small talk and going over and over all my issues. But when I got there, there was a table full of instructor/education friends with balloons, noise makers and really bad (and yes, sometimes raunchy) jokes. It was such a nice time – they really perked me up. I guess the nicest part was knowing how much other people care.*

Another invaluable help for preserving the sanity of the caretaker is provided by Medicare. If the patient is on hospice care, Medicare will provide a five-day respite stay for the hospice patient in an inpatient facility or other type of 24-hour a day nursing facility, thereby giving the caregiver a total break away from the worry and stress, and helping to relieve some of the caregiver stress. Medicare will pay 100% for this stay. There is always reliable care and support from the hospice team.

Feb 7/99 - I wish I knew what our timing was on all this . . .We did the big shower routine yesterday. He did fine (and I did too). If he were to fall, I'm not sure what I'd do. The way he staggers into the bathroom, I worry that may come someday . . .He has agreed that we should probably call hospice. I need help with his plugged ear, plugged nose, bed sore (it's getting better because he's sleeping on his other side) and feet. There's probably way more that I don't even know about. He's hardly eating anything anymore.

Feb 13/99 - He's having a hard time concentrating. Sometimes when he's talking he closes his eyes as he's struggling for the right thought. Sometimes he says things that make absolutely no sense at all, and I have to ask questions to help him figure out what he was trying to say. We did the famous shower today. I wrote down the timing of what we did --it took from 4:15 to almost 6:00 from start to finish. He'd sit up then lie down, get up and eat a few slices of apple, then lie down, sit up, stand up and walk around the foot of the bed, sit on edge of bed where we switched oxygen supplies so he's using liquid from the large tank and gas from the green portable tank, lie down. Finally walks into the shower where he sits on the stool several minutes before we even complete undressing him. And on and on. At least it's one more week that we made it work.

Feb 20/99 - . . . Steve and Renee came. We had a really good time--Gary was in the best mood he's been in a long time – he was joking and saying funny things . . . Gary's bed sore still looks ugly. Its scabbed portion seems to be a bit smaller, but there's a large red area around it, especially if he's been lying on that side. I was terrified that it was infected – it looks that bad. I've been rubbing "bag balm" on it--that's supposed to be the best thing. Gary did talk about calling hospice a few weeks ago. Now I find I'm the one resisting the call. I could use their expertise on things like the bed sore, but I keep thinking we really are bumbling along okay. I haven't made any major mistakes so far (except for the bed sore). I wonder if maybe I'm afraid to call them in because they will point out to me all of the things I have been doing wrong. I worry about how I'll deal with the end--and if I'll know what's the right thing to do then.

I GUESS THIS REALLY IS HAPPENING TO US

"We cannot let go of anything we do not accept," says meditation teacher Stephen Levine. "The fear which has always guarded these heavy emotions . . . . becomes an ally which whispers that we are coming to our edge, to unplumbed depths, to the space in which all growth occurs.''[24]

> Feb 24/99 - . . . Camille, the hospice nurse who came before Christmas . . . came again yesterday morning. She got us all signed on and as she left, she said she thought it would all be over in a couple of weeks--give or take a few days. That was a reality check for me I wasn't prepared for. I knew it would be soon, but I thought we had <u>months</u>, not weeks . . . The doctor had prescribed an anxiety pill and some morphine. I gave Gary the anxiety pill about 5:30 which knocked him out for two hours. At bedtime I gave him both pills-- and he slept until morning . . . he called me at about 7:45. He said he was feeling better, but he was all goofy and spacey . . . He went back to bed, the nurse's aide came and we washed his hair. . . I gave him the two meds again--and that's all she wrote! He was in and out of dead sleep and semi-consciousness. . . . whenever he woke up, he complained about the meds and how they made him feel. When I was giving him his regular meds that he's been taking for years, he was very suspicious about each one and what it might do. I finally backed off one of the pills and promised him he didn't need to take anything he didn't want.

Hospice was an omni-present part of our lives from this day on. Some of the people who came were great and some were not so great. A young volunteer who had lost a child came to counsel us on grief. As well-meaning as she was, I could not identify with her or her situation. A kindly clergyman came asking us if we needed any spiritual support. I thanked him, but told him we were okay. A young woman came to give Gary a sponge bath. She also was very well-meaning, but I found it necessary to protect Gary's privacy. But they were there, and they were willing to be there.

We clicked with a favorite nurse who proved to be a God-send. The first thing she did was bring in a large adhesive bandage that she slapped over the bed sore. Within two days the bed sore was drying up and healing. She was polite but kind of tsk-tsked at my bag-balm remedy. She helped greatly with balancing the meds. She, or another registered nurse, was on call around the clock just for us.

> Feb 25/99 - Gary was very insistent this morning that he did not want to spend his last days in a fog like he had yesterday. So I gave him just the

---

[24] Stephen Levine as quoted in the McLeod book, p 136

morphine. It seemed to help him rest, but he was also lucid . . . I somehow think this is not going to go easy. I envisioned that he would slip away in his sleep. But after today I think he's going to resist up to the end. He told me today that he's done with the history--that I can finish it. And he's said goodbye to David. I don't know what he has left. I only know he wants to be totally conscious and lucid for whatever it is.

The Friday before Gary died he dictated a beautiful letter to each of the kids. He talked to all of the grandkids, and told them how important it was for them to pick good friends, to go to church and to listen to their parents. He called his long-time friend in Tennessee and told him goodbye. Gary was very calm, but I could tell his friend was having a very difficult time. His brother, Rich, called and they talked for just a few moments but they told each other how much they loved each other. He put forth a grand effort to finish all he had to do.

Feb 28/99 - I thought Gary would go last night. He woke up and called to me. I helped him and as I was rolling him back he said, "I really need to go. I can't hold out much longer." I told him he was finished with his work, that he'd worked very hard the day before and had gotten it all done. I told him we'd had a great ride. And he said, "We made a great family and that was what was important." He thanked me, then pulled up his face mask to give me a kiss.

March 1/99 - It's 10:46 PM on Monday, March 1. Gary is still alive. He is breathing so loudly I jump when his breathing gets shallow. His heart is beating today at 104/minute—last week it was 56/minute. His pulse looks like it is ready to jump out of his throat. I've kept him pretty drugged today, but earlier he pulled me down to him and said "goodbye." I told him to have a good trip and save me a place. He smirked, and said he would. Later on he started complaining about the light. He said "turn off the light." I told him the blinds were down and no lights were on. He said it looked like the sun, then he said something about the sun with clouds on it. I called Val so she could hear it. She said "Go towards the light, Daddy. It's all right." He said, "It's not that easy. I don't know how." Val told him to let the light come to him. Then he said something about the door being closed. I told Val to open the doors, but I don't think that's what he meant.

March 3/99 - Gary died yesterday at 6:40 PM. I cannot believe it is over. He is gone. It is all over. The hospice nurse had come in the morning to help me change him and make him more comfortable . . . she helped me get him cleaned up and in new pajamas. He was groaning a lot, and the

nurse told me I shouldn't feel guilty giving him the maximum meds –
every hour . . . he was moaning and groaning and mumbling
unintelligibly except for one time when we heard him say "in the name of
Jesus Christ."

He was praying at the end. Our favorite nurse came later and told us to gather everyone. The person who is dying cannot do it alone—the caregiver cannot do it alone. So she was there assisting us through to the end—telling us that what was happening was normal so we wouldn't be afraid. The girls and I were there on the bed singing hymns to him. And then—he was gone.

Just like that.

And it was all over—the funeral plans needed to be made. Did I do enough? If I had done more and had done it better would he have lived longer?

My days, weeks and months as a caregiver were over--just over. Was it appropriate to feel relieved? To feel the lifting of the burden? I did—and then I felt guilty for feeling that way.

Dr. Barbara Wheeler states in her book *When a Spouse Dies*, "Why wouldn't relief be an expected, normal response? It's no news that caretaking is one of the most difficult jobs on the planet. Most caretakers who were interviewed said they willingly, without second thought, stepped up to the task. 'I did it for him—not out of duty,' one woman explained. 'Love and commitment go a long way,' she added. 'But I'm exhausted—physically and emotionally.'" Dr. Wheeler goes on to say, "Further kudos to these caretakers for having the courage and honesty to express their conflicted emotional anguish!"[25]

The physical dependency on me had ended, but the emotional impact would carry for a long time--a very long time. Author McLeod says "Caregiving reveals how assuming the care of a dependent loved one has the potential to alter us at the core of our being, opening our heart's capacity to live fully even in the midst of loss."[26]

---

[25] Barbara R. Wheeler, <u>When a Spouse Dies</u> (Springville: Cedar Fort, Inc. 2012) p 22
[26] Wheeler, p 23

There had to be important things that I had learned from experiencing this dying process. What were they?

I learned the importance of having a "good death" where the dying person has passed on his burdens--both emotional and physical--where the necessary reconciliations have been made--and there is peace. And where all that is left now is for the *dying time* to become *a spiritual time*. Where the patient has not only made reconciliations with those on earth, but has reconciled all differences with his God—and there is peace.

Caring for my dying husband was probably one of the most overwhelming and emotional challenges of my life. Do I love Gary more now than I did before? I would say—yes! It is through the gift of service that your love grows.

Action Items for This Chapter:

(1) Keep your "I Love You's" up to date.
(2) Create your Advance Directive or POLST
(3) Create your Health Care Proxy
(4) Reconcile your worries and troubles, make amends, ask for forgiveness.
(5) Hold onto each other as if your *death* depended on it.

CHAPTER SIX

IT DOESN'T GET BETTER, IT JUST GETS DIFFERENT
--or--GRIEVING DEATH

⟨∿⟩

Once again, I would remind the reader that I am not a professional therapist. In this chapter on dealing with grief I can only share what I learned through my own research and interviews, and from my personal thoughts and experiences.

Whether the death of your spouse has been long expected or whether it has been sudden, the shock to mind and soul is almost unbearable. The grief is so palpable you do not know what to do or how to do it. Others hover around you and over you, asking questions, waiting for answers. There are so many decisions--and they all need to be made right now. [Refer to the APPENDIX for a list of those items that need to be addressed after your spouse's death.]

Have funeral plans been discussed and those sensitive decisions already made? Yes? Did you decide on having a living trust or a will—and the papers have been drawn up and signed? Yes? Do you know where all (or most) of the papers are? Yes? How easy for you!

124

It is easy--provided the work has been done and the choices have already been finalized by you *and your spouse*. With those decisions made, hopefully all that's left for you now—is to mourn.

Before you can catch your breath, the funeral is over. Everyone goes back to their homes and their lives. All except you. As you walk into your door after the funeral, truly alone for the first time, you are going back to a life that has been forever changed. Your home and your surroundings—even though not disturbed--have been forever changed. Your family is different, your friends are different. The workplace is different. You are left trying to cope with your loss and, at the same time, cope with a life that will never be the same.

> *March 4/99 – I know millions of women have lost their husbands---I don't know how you survive the agony. I have been scrambling today – buying some new clothes, returning the oxygen equipment, and such. Every once in a while something happens or I see something, and I lose it. I saw his leftovers in the fridge, and my heart felt like it would break—it actually hurt. I have his pillow with his scent still on it – I wonder how long it will last.*

The initial shock lasts for quite a while. But eventually and very slowly you accept the reality that this has, indeed, happened to you and you concede that life will never be the same. From the moment you knew your spouse had died, you understood within your very being that from this instant on your life would be altered and changed in ways you probably could not imagine. Where you were part of a couple, now you are single. Just this simple fact has so many ramifications to it.

There are so many things you need to think about and do. But for a few days, all you want to do is to be alone--if you possibly can.

> *March 7/99 - It's Sunday and all I've done mostly is sleep--and think. I've only had two phone calls—one from Val and one from Lynne. I'll take next week off. I'd like to take the following week off also but I don't know--I'll have to see. I've been surprised at how calm I've been most of the day—as though I'd been alone for a long time. Eating alone was strange and I did go into Gary's bed to finish watching a TV show. Yesterday after the funeral, I was saddened that on Gary's pillow I couldn't smell his scent any longer. Today I've been able to detect it slightly. It's amazing what comfort it gives me. I know now why widows and widowers find it*

difficult to put away the deceased's belongings. It's because you don't want to forget, and you are afraid you might if you put or give things away. I know I don't want to forget—-you can't go through what we (I) did and not be changed by it. I want to remember the promises I made to him. I have also got to get on with my life as a single person. I'm a widow—and I'm single. And for the first time in 62 years, I'm all alone. All alone!

This is the time for you to repair from this traumatic shock to your very being. It is important that for the next few weeks you take very good care, even selfish care, of yourself. Now is the time to pamper yourself, and if that means telling others to ("please") leave you alone, just do it. The emotional devastation is overwhelming and can do a lot of damage if you are not careful to safeguard your best interests.

March 8/99 - I took one of Gary's Lorazapam last night. It said on the bottle it was the same dosage as what my doctor had prescribed for me, but it surely seemed to have more punch. It knocked me into a blissful sleep—until 10:30 this morning, I was very tired and groggy, but did run a few errands, then came back and slept <u>soundly</u> for two more hours. I've just taken one of my prescriptions—I'll see how I am in the morning. I seem to be functioning mostly in a fog—or by rote. I have TONS of paperwork to do, and I know that stuff is piling up at work. And really all I want to do is sleep. It all needs to be done, but I can't face it. I feel all tight inside. I can't cry, except for a very few sobs that gulp up at unexplained moments. I still smell the pillow—it does give comfort in an odd unexplained way.

I hated leaving the house, because then I always needed to come back home. Maybe I had a few hours of distraction, but coming home and walking in the door was filled with despair. Gary was not there to greet me and give me a kiss. He was not there to hold me--ever again.

Whenever I heard a noise outside, I expected him to walk in the door. And then I would realize that he would never again, himself, walk in that back door. The emptiness was tangible.

March 11/99 - Went to town today—made a payment on the remainder of the bill at the mortuary ($6700+ and I will still owe additional for a headstone), went into work just to say hello—(oh, I'm not anxious to go back, but may go back on Tuesday)--got gas, went to the grocery store. The minute I walked in the back door I started to sob—it was walking into *an empty house and not having Gary there in the bedroom. I'm not feeling well tonight—somewhat queasy—I hope I'm not getting the flu. It would serve me right. I've been writing thank you notes all this evening—I've been doing the hardest ones that require some thought and emotion. Maybe by tomorrow I can do the ones that are mostly just "thanks." I really wish I could stay away from work for a full month. No such luck.*

Right after Gary died, the grieving was almost the easiest. I was mostly alone those first few weeks which allowed the tears to flow unencumbered. I didn't need to worry about embarrassing myself or embarrassing anyone else around me with my histrionics. The gulping and gasping were quite liberating, and I was free to express my sorrow and anguish.

Scientific studies have proven the cathartic aspects of tears. Wonderful chemicals are released in the brain during crying that help the body to adapt to emotional stresses.[27] We all know the benefits of a "good cry." And I had plenty of those.

I was crying for myself, mostly. I was crying tears of frustration over the enormity of what was left to do. I was crying over the unfairness (to us both) of it all. I was crying mostly out of self-pity. I was desperately sorry for myself.

Only the very dearest and safest people in my life (one or two close friends and my two daughters) were surrounding me at this time, and they understood. Well---I think.

And then they were gone. And I wasn't ready for them to be gone. My boss expected me back at work. I had told him that I wanted to retire, but he wouldn't let me. He told me it would be good for me to work for another year. So I went back to work (which, in the long run, turned out to be the very thing I needed to do).

My friends at work were very dear, but they didn't know how to act toward me. A weeping widow is about as much fun as the plague. They were clearly uncomfortable and wondering how I would react now that my life was so significantly different. Would I be the administrator/manager I had been--exacting, positive, in control, or would I be delicate and weepy? What they didn't know is that it was both. I was back doing my job, but was fighting tears much of the time. It was a good trick to maintain the control.

---

[27] Joyce Brothers, <u>Widowed</u> (New York: Ballantine, 1990) p 68

There are many reasons why you feel you cannot face others. One is having to answer that dreaded, inane question, "How are you doing?" Of course you are not doing well. What are you going to say? "I've just had my heart torn out—how the heck do you think I am?"

I developed a little trick of answering that question with another question. In my response I would say, "Well, how are you?" It's easy, it's clean, and it lets everyone off the hook. You haven't had to disclose how awful you are feeling, and the asker of the question doesn't have to listen to how awful you are. It is a win/win for everyone.

After the death of her ex-spouse, and when my daughter would be asked that same unanswerable question, she would answer, "It depends on the day." It's a non-committal comment to a question no-one really wants the answer to.

Another reason you cannot bear to face others, and probably the most prevalent reason, is having others tell you how to grieve: "Just plunge back into life and get on with the program!" "Get back to work as soon as you can!" "Get yourself busy and it will get your mind off your problems!" "Go to church—you will find the help you need there." "Don't stay alone all the time---you need to be out with other people!"[28]

There are many well-meaning folks trying to tell you how you should be getting back to a normal life. They mean to be helpful, but unless and until they have experienced a loss such as yours, they have no idea—no understanding of where you are and what you are going through! Common sense tells others that if you can get your mind off your grief, you will heal faster. But you know that is not the case.

The pain of grief needs to be fully experienced. The grief is there, it is not going away (no matter how hard you try to mask it or forget it), it needs to be faced, and it needs to be dealt with—by yourself, in your own way and time. You are the one and the only one who can decide how to grieve and how long it is going to take.

It has been fourteen years since my husband's death, and I am still shocked by a song or a memory that still brings up a tear—though they are mostly mellow tears. Even so, sometimes when I remember the last tedious months, I cry more than tender tears.

---

[28] Grief Resources/Understanding Death/10 Common Myths. Retrieved 10 Feb 2013 from www.nfda.org

Does that mean I am still grieving? I would imagine so, but I don't know.

> *March 13/99 - Today has been the first day I have felt "lonely." I slept until 10:00, had breakfast and read the paper, and then I climbed into Gary's bed and slept on and off until about 1:00. I took a sleeping pill (again) last night (and I just now took another one). I didn't take one Thursday night, and ended up taking one about 2:30 a.m. and not going to sleep until about 4:00. It was a mess—I don't want to get hooked on them, but I can't sleep otherwise. I transcribed more of Gary's history today and wrote more thank you cards—and cried, a lot.*

After the shock and the acceptance that you are truly alone, and after you have hopefully had the time to withdraw from society and have taken some personal healing time, then comes the time when you begin to restructure your life as a single person. For all of your married years, you lived mirroring yourself and your thoughts and ideas against those of your spouse. You asked questions of your spouse and you expected thoughtful and well-reasoned answers. You identified yourself as being one of two people. The two of you were considered to be a "two-some."

Once you have lost that identity as a married person--it died upon the death of your spouse--you are now required to reinvent yourself into a different and unique person, to re-create a new self—a new normal. The dynamics are quite different. Where you were two, now you are one. And beware, you *will* be treated differently, whether you are a woman or a man. I suppose the widower is seen as being more helpless and needing more assistance. The casseroles keep coming longer to him, and he gets invited by old friends out to dinner and other entertainments.

The widow's situation is quite different. A widow has lost her social prestige of "having a man." In all probability, she is in a different economic situation than before. It is extremely difficult for the widow *not* to consider herself as being in a lower status as others feel "sorry" for her.

Except for rare instances, she no longer gets included in the same couples' groups that she and her husband were part of. When I suddenly realized that old groups of friends were going on without me, I questioned a wife of one of the groups who was a very close friend and who I knew would tell me the truth. She was very embarrassed as she told me that some of the other wives were concerned that their husbands might now look upon me with different eyes and the wives would rather I not be included anymore.

At 62 years old and with that amount of mileage on my body and my face, this piece of information left me stunned! All I could do was feel angry towards these people. At a time when I needed the most support I could get, they would retreat from me and forget their heartfelt promises to "give me whatever help I needed."

And then one afternoon, the husband of one of my friends showed up unannounced at my door to see if I needed some help— and then a little more help. All I could think was, oh come on now-- is this really happening? Fortunately he left easily, especially when he could see how stupefied I was. Interestingly enough, I have since learned, many times over, that I am not the only widow who has this same story to tell.[29]

I did begin to realize that socially I was odd-woman out. Fortunately there was a small handful of very dear and devoted couples who didn't forget me and who would call and include me in their plans. To them I will be forever grateful.

Hospice was also invaluable at this time. The hospice staff was in constant touch with me one way or another. For the first several months I received phone calls and almost weekly mailings from them--comforting me, answering my questions, participating in my grief.

One of the most tender mailings I received from them was a large envelope. Inside were two large paper butterflies, hand-painted and glittered. They had been made by children who were also grieving, and who shared their grief with me in this giving-way.

Hospice was not telling me how to grieve—the personnel were there for me in my grief. One of the most valuable pieces of information they gave me was very practical: do not sell my home or make any significant financial decisions before a year has passed. Following the most climactic change in my life, there was a great urge to want to make other drastic changes—mostly for the purpose of sweeping away all the distress of the past year.

Rabbi Earl Grollman advises: "You may be tempted to make a radical change in your life--to sell your house, to move someplace different, to make a fresh start, away from your familiar home and all the painful memories. Wait awhile. The time is not right for major

---

[29] Brothers, p 82

decisions. Your judgment is still uncertain. You are still in horrible pain. Getting used to a new life takes time, thought and patience."[30]

Newer research now advises the surviving spouse to not make any major decisions for at least *two years*. Psychiatrist David Ranks, affiliated with the Intermountain Medical Center in Salt Lake City, Utah, states that around the second anniversary of the death of the spouse, there is a physical and emotional reliving of the death and grief experience that results in a rebirth of the original debilitating stresses and sorrows. The surviving spouse is, therefore, subject to the same risk for illness and death that would have been possible immediately on the death of the spouse. Understanding this possibility and, perhaps, preparing for it can save fundamental mistakes.[31]

So life kept going on. My son, David, started smoking again (after many years of abstinence). I began to gain weight, again. If there was no stress, I would certainly create it--which I am sure led to a lowered immune system, which eventually led to a second back surgery a few years later. If there was a cold, I caught it. If someone had the flu, I caught it. And stress? It was there, just waiting for me.

Many times I had a sense of Gary calling me in the middle of the night. I would wake up with a start, begin to jump out of bed, and then would realize I had been dreaming. It was most unsettling because it was so real. I never had the sense that he was present in the room (as I know other people have experienced), but my dreams were extremely vivid. Twelve years later Gary is still a very distinct presence in my dreams (but he is no longer calling for my help).

March 14/99 It happened again this morning---it was about 7:45 and I heard Gary call me—just as clear as he did 100 times before. I started to leap out of bed (like 100 times before), then I realized where I was--and he was.

I kept getting invited to support groups, but I couldn't imagine exposing my personal devastation to strangers. How could an assemblage of people who didn't know me (and I didn't know them) understand what I was experiencing and have any compassion for me—and vice versa?

---

[30] Victor Parachin, "Grief Relief", <u>The Director</u> Aug 2001
[31] David Ranks, personal conversation, 13 Sept. 2012

But don't write off support groups just because I did. Many report the benefits of participating in support groups--the sharing of emotions and feelings which are facilitated by a professional grief counselor. And many years later I have learned from experience-- from now being in a support group myself--that people do understand and can offer the encouragement that you need. But groups don't work for everyone; you will need to make your own decision on that one. [32]

It is extremely difficult for most people to reach out and ask for help. This presents a strange dichotomy in that this is the time you are most in need of help and understanding, and yet this is the time when you are trying valiantly to go it alone.

The flood of original support slowly dwindles and disappears. Others assume you are okay after a certain length of time, and the support ends before you are ready for it to end. It seemed I could freely express my grief to my daughters. In a role reversal, they had become the mothers (the nurturers). I became the child, going to them for comfort and healing. I was taking from them, not realizing nor admitting that they were grieving as well (does a child grieve for a parent differently than one does for a spouse?). I had lost sight of the fact that they were also desolate, and I was not very supportive of them in their own suffering.

It all changed after about a year. Life was now supposed to be back to normal. I was expected to be the mom again and go back to giving the usual "mom support." As said earlier, everyone goes back to their own lives—except the remaining spouse.

LONELINESS and ANGER

Loneliness is a constant. I had the benefit of going to a job every day, being surrounded by people who were, for the most part, very pleasant and fun to be around. But I was lonely even when surrounded by people. The void was too deep--and wasn't healed over.

I had lost half of my life--my long-time companion and friend. The yearning to have him back again was solid and real. The

---

[32] Victor Parachin, "10 Common Myths & Realities about Grief" The Director May 1999

companionship wasn't all I wanted to have back--I wanted the security of a marriage, I wanted the "couple" way of life, I didn't want to feel alienated any more from the world.

Loneliness is part of the transition of grief, and if there are no other family members in the home, the loneliness can become painful and unbearable. Because of an already lowered immune system, the loneliness can cause serious physical problems for a surviving spouse. Widows and widowers are vulnerable to serious diseases and illnesses. Combine this with the loneliness that also results from being cut off from prior social groups, and the results can be devastating.

It's an unbelievable fact that many widowers live only a very few months after the death of their wives. It's interesting to think of why this might be so. Could it be that the husband has been so dependent on his wife for the very basics of living--cooking, laundry, cleaning, shopping, etc.--that he doesn't know how to take care of himself? And he ultimately gets sick and dies?

Could it be that he has lost the social skills to create a new life, and he is so lonely that he decides that rather than living alone, he might as well die? Could it be that because of religious and spiritual beliefs of a life's existence after death, and that if his belief is that he can be with his sweetheart again, he loses his will to live?

Statistics prove that the bereaved person's immune system is extremely low, thereby making him or her subject to many illnesses and diseases. Lack of sleep, stress and fatigue are most common during a time like this. Often we hear of a husband or wife dying either simultaneously or within a very short period of each other. Dying of a "broken heart" is not just a romantic notion; it is a very real consequence.

I can understand wanting to give up and die. There were many times I was wishing I could die, or not minding if I were to die. What an easy way out.

Soon after Gary died I was called by a very well-meaning older member of my church inviting me to a group of "singles" who get together and socialize. "You are one of us now, you know," I swore she cackled as she said that. I didn't go.

For some people anger can become a ready emotion because it seems to be such a natural part of grief. Because we are so conscious of doing things right, we find it unbelievable that we could (or

133

should) be angry. But the anger boils readily below the surface, waiting to erupt--waiting to explode in a variety of ways and toward a variety of individuals.

We are mad at the doctors who should have been smart enough to save our spouse from dying; at insensitive people who make stupid remarks; at couples we see enjoying themselves in the restaurant, the movie theatre, in the park. We are mad at the world in general; mad at God for allowing this to happen; mad because we feel guilty for being mad.

Sometimes I was furiously angry with Gary for dying. I would scream at him and curse him (through my tears). This would usually happen after I found myself in a mess of some kind, a mess that he usually would have handled. One day I was driving up to my cabin, slipping and sliding precariously away from drop-off cliffs in mud seven inches deep, screaming angry curses at Gary at the top of my lungs. Under normal circumstances he would have (1) talked me out of going, and/or (2) would have been doing the driving himself. Here I was in this mess that I had created for myself but had to blame on someone else. Sometimes I just got mad and yelled at him for having the nerve to die and for screwing up my life by leaving me alone.

In the book *Surviving Grief*, Dr. Sanders writes, "Anger is a difficult emotion to express in bereavement, because we feel that we are under the close scrutiny of others. We want to do things correctly and set a good example. But we are the most important persons during this time, and we need to take care of ourselves, especially now. Our own needs should be our top priority. When we take care of ourselves, we set the best example of all." [33]

March 21/99 - Time goes so fast! Two weeks since the funeral. For the first time, I have felt today like moving forward. Mark and David came today—put my bed in the basement, moved Gary's bedroom furniture into the front bedroom and switched other furniture into the back BR for an office. It has been a busy, positive day with much getting done, and much still to be done. I find myself having to think of Gary and remember. And as I make these changes and get rid of his stuff, I wonder if that will happen more. I can't think that it would—I still find myself sniffing his pillow a couple of times a day, and it still gives me reassurance.

---

[33] Catherine M. Sanders, <u>Surviving Grief</u> (New York: Wiley & Sons, Inc., 1992)   p 62

Cleaning out the room--cleaning *Gary* out of the room--was one of the most painful aspects of the process. The medical equipment was thrown away or put in boxes to be returned. Cleaning his shirts and pants out of the closets was doable, but I could not clean the socks and underwear out of the dresser drawers. Doing that was too personal—it was as though he were dying all over again. I had to leave the room as Lynne and Valerie did the cleaning.

> *March 26/99 - I started cleaning some of Gary's stuff and lost it. Maybe I'm pushing too fast and not taking enough time. I almost feel as though I'm dishonoring him to move out his stuff. I want to get on, but I don't.*

A friend of mine once stated that cleaning out her husband's shoes was the most difficult thing for her to do. She said it was the finality that they could never go anywhere, again.[34]

I got more angry as I cleaned out these final remnants. I suppose being mad was my way of dealing with packing his clothes away in garbage bags to be donated to charity. Is this what is left of a decent, righteous man's life--to be packed away in thick, black, plastic garbage bags? What disdain and dishonor to his memory!

SPIRITUALITY

Even if not religiously affiliated, most people, while grieving the death of a loved one, still tend to want a relationship with some kind of higher power or higher existence. Losing a spouse (or anyone close, for that matter) makes us want to have answers—answers about what life is. What is its meaning, where did we come from, where are we going? What is this struggle all about? What can this death possibly mean to those of us who are being left behind?

We want the answers to why a dear one had to die right now, or had to die in a particularly tragic way, or had to die so young, or--had to die at all. We beg for some kind of meaning to it all. We cry and wonder if there really is a God who could be so cruel.

In search of those answers, most of us rely on the beliefs and the religion of our childhood (and, hopefully, adulthood). We rely on the

---

[34] Joan Didion, <u>The Year of Magical Thinking</u> (New York: Vintage, 2005) p 36

strengths we can receive from those early convictions of faith. And those original beliefs and principles make us resilient and capable of moving forward. Our religion and spiritual philosophies usually determine the type of funeral to be had, the music to be sung, the eulogies to be given and by whom, the prayers to be said. These are the traditions and rituals that are comforting and bring peace to the family and friends of the deceased.

And there is always the power of prayer. In her book *When a Spouse Dies*, Dr. Barbara R. Wheeler states: "Those whose faith in God has been a part of their lives . . . emphasized how helpful their beliefs were during their traumatic loss. Prayer--communication with God--seemed to take on an even more significant meaning at this time . . . All who acknowledged their belief in God reported the sense of His omnipresence on a daily basis, guiding them through their bereavement---a feeling of being 'carried.'"[35]

Those of us who have lived through the death of a loved one tend to look at our life—or what's left of it—differently. There's nothing more poignant or emotional than watching your loved one pass from this life. How disheartening it would be to think that there was no place for him or her to pass "to." How daunting to think that this is the end and that there is no more. It is that "more" that give us purpose, that gives us that meaning we are hungering for, that gives us the answers.

Some of us more easily foster the seeds of spirituality from which we gain our strength. Psychiatrist, Dr. Elisabeth Kubler-Ross, has found that women "who have gone through a lot of difficulties in life reach a certain degree of acceptance and serenity. They know that death is a part of life, and they take it with incredible serenity and peace."[36] How comforting to be in that place.

For others it may be more difficult--particularly those who seek a logical and scientific explanation towards the issues of life and death. They will find their own way and their own justifications as to what this death means. They will find their own path to a life of calmness and serenity---and acceptance.

But for those of us who do believe, being able to rely on divine guidance and the strengths from our Lord offers us tranquility, understanding, acceptance--and finally peace.

---

[35] Barbara Wheeler, <u>When a Spouse Dies</u>, (Utah, Plain Sight Publishing) p 42
[36] Kubler-Ross as found in Brothers p 67

ANNIVERSARIES

The first year of loss is the roughest, because many of the holiday traditions and customs of a family have evolved and been practiced for decades as an intact family. It is amazing what a vacant space is left after the death of an integral family member--especially the dad or the mom.

Grief counselor and instructor, Dr. Barbara R. Wheeler states, "Under ordinary circumstances, holidays magnify everything. For those struggling with loss, the intensity can be overwhelming as we search for ways to get through it all. I am not quite ready to acknowledge that Valentine's Day is anything more than just another day. I cope by ignoring it. *Denial is not unhealthy as long as I am consciously aware of the choice I've made.*"[37]

Mother's Day was the first holiday I had to face, but my children took care of that, making certain that I was well remembered. A very few days later was mine and Gary's wedding anniversary. It was a beautiful spring day in May, and I told my kids that all I wanted to do was go to the cemetery and spend my anniversary with Gary--which is exactly what I did. The winds were barely a refreshing spring breeze and carried the fragrance of the emerging lilacs that bordered the cemetery. I first fussed with the flowers I had brought, putting them in water in the vase that was part of the headstone. I sat down on the ground absorbing the surroundings of the spring day, the goodbye to a harsh and bitter winter and the agonies it had brought, the promise of better days to come. I wept, maybe even wailed a bit, but the young men could not hear me over the drone of the mowers as they were preparing the lawns for Memorial Day.

Christmas was the very worst holiday! I dreaded even preparing for this day because of all the traditions we had created over the years. Granted, as each of my kids now had their own families, things had changed and we had already adapted to new situations. But this was different--this was going to require more than adapting.

Then Valerie invited me to come to her home to have Christmas with her young family. I could not have been more delighted. After all, what's better than Christmas with little children? To see the happiness and wonder in their faces at the marvel of the Santa Claus

---

[37] Wheeler, p 29

magic, to experience their mercenary selfishness of why there isn't more, and to try to help during the melt-downs brought on by hunger and fatigue. It took me right back to past Christmas mornings with my own little ones--pure delight!

The first year of holidays, birthdays and anniversaries is the hardest because things are not the same, and never will be again. It's amazing what the absence of that one person can mean to just that one day. It's as if a play has been staged for each of the holidays, and this person has played a major leading role for years and years for all to see and experience (and enjoy). And now that actor is suddenly gone, and all the other actors have had to change their marks on-stage and ad-lib their lines in order to save the show. And after a few trials that didn't go so well, suddenly the play is intact again. The show goes on!

RESTORATIVE ATTITUDES, ALTITUDES and RESOLUTION

You don't wake up one day and suddenly realize you are no longer grieving. It doesn't work that way. But some days you wake up and seem to have a little sunnier outlook on the day. Some days you wake up and realize that you haven't been hurting. That's not to say that you haven't been thinking about or remembering your spouse. It's that you haven't been hurting when you remembered.

In actuality, remembering helps in the healing. Sigmund Freud said that each time you remember, it's as though a healing film grows over the memory and the memory is no longer an open wound. Tears and remembering are both integral parts of the healing process. Eventually the new life begins to take over--there is finally a subtle admission that you are alone and that, no matter *what*, you are going to continue to be alone. You don't have to like it, but there will be certain aspects of this new identity that begin to feel better and more comfortable so that it isn't so painful or foreign to you.

Your habits will change and you might begin to like some of your new rituals--such as your ritual for going to bed. Maybe you never watched TV in bed at night (or in the morning) because your spouse couldn't stand it. Well, now you can. Maybe you can have the section of the newspaper without having to relinquish first choices to your spouse. You can fold the paper any way you want;

you can be the first to fill out the crossword puzzle. Perhaps you can now listen to *your* music--country all the way, no more classical!

When you are out with friends, laughing riotously and having a good time, don't feel guilty or think you are being unfaithful or disloyal to your spouse's memory. That is exactly where your spouse would want you to be--having a good time and getting on with your life.

But be aware, there will always be those ungenerous folks who will try to make you feel guilty that you are, perhaps, not being respectful enough over the death of your spouse, that you are out enjoying yourself too soon, that you are not wearing the "widow's weeds" (aka: grieving and suffering) long enough.

REMARRIAGE?

And what about remarriage? In spite of all the bravado of "going it alone" and "being your own person," there is nothing worse than longing to be held tightly and firmly in another's arms--longing for that wonder of sharing another's love. But without some preplanning and thinking into the future, there could easily be unanticipated and disappointing consequences that could undermine the hoped-for happiness of a new marriage.

A younger surviving spouse may be more inclined to perceive a future filled with promise and anticipation, and is probably more inclined to actively seek another partner. There may still be young children to be raised, and financial difficulties that could be solved with a second breadwinner. Having someone to play and make plans with is an exciting prospect.

Older survivors may be more set in their ways and more hesitant to make the adjustments and adaptations that having a new spouse would require. There may be a greater reluctance to care for another ailing spouse, which could be a reality in a marriage between older couples. With elders relying on Social Security and pension incomes, half of those funds could be relinquished through a remarriage. And the fear always prevails that a dear one could be taken again, way too soon. But the desire and basic need for companionship and affection is so powerful that it's easy (or easier) to ignore the negatives and to want to plunge forward into a new relationship.

Interestingly enough, if a surviving spouse has had a positive, fulfilling marriage, he or she is more likely to rebound, maybe too quickly, into a new marriage. Or, sometimes, genuine overpowering loneliness spurs rash action that has not been well reasoned. If the grieving process after the death of a spouse has not been completed, or nearly completed, problems and disillusionments can develop.

As previously discussed, now that you are alone after having been half of a couple, by default you now build a new identity as a single person. At this point there is no choice--you *are* a single person. If you go quickly into a new marriage bringing the same aspirations and expectations as from your previous marriage, and if you are still essentially the same person (still a spouse) as you originally were, there is the danger of bringing into the new marriage the ghosts of the marriage-past that can loom omnipresent to the new spouse and threaten the new union.

Author Dr. Barbara Wheeler states that "Marrying out of loneliness is a red flag. Learning to accept and manage aloneness comes first. Readiness is also dependent upon moving past grief and possible guilt."[38]

The blending of two families is another potential problem. This means not only merging children, it can mean dealing with multiple homes, furniture, personal belongings, financial assets and other individual properties--some valuable, some not.

In facing the possible remarriage of a parent, the children may--realistically or not--feel that you are being disloyal to the deceased parent. They may also fear a loss of your love and affection that will now be shared with someone else. And with older children, an overpowering supposition is that they may feel they are at jeopardy of losing their inheritance. If the adult children of one or the other spouses (or both) feel disenfranchised (read: "disinherited"), they can and will make life miserable for everyone as they let their disapproval of the union be known.

It is natural that spouses in the new marriage want to assure that their own children are protected and that monies destined for them will not, through lack of preplanning (or wicked step-mother/step-father actions), be side-tracked to other areas, namely the children of the new spouse.

Some preplanning and forethought before any marriage takes place can help to prevent issues of jealousy and resentfulness among the merged families. One of those plans could be a pre-nuptial

---

[38] Wheeler, p 87

agreement. This agreement is entered into before the marriage making an accounting of the assets going into the marriage and defining what is to happen to those assets upon the death (or divorce) of either of the parties. This document can also take into account children from a previous marriage and can address their issues.

Another plan could be the establishment of a living trust or a will where, as with the prenuptial agreement, the assets of each partner coming to the new marriage are identified and decisions are legally made (prior to the marriage) as to how and when all personal assets will be distributed. These two legal processes can result in the same outcomes, though the procedures differ. If the couple lives in a community property state, those state laws should also be addressed.

In order to be fully protected, each partner should have his or her own attorney. This is the only way to guard the individual family needs of each partner.

A 1995 AARP workbook "Think of your Future" gives some guidelines to help a couple determine if they are ready to remarry.

- *Have you been widowed or divorced at least two years?*
- *Have you built a sustaining and full life for yourself alone?*
- *Are you happy with your current life?*
- *Have you known your potential spouse at least six months and do you feel you know each other well?*
- *Are you both willing, where it is appropriate, to give up your present homes and make a new life together in a new housing arrangement?*
- *Will your joint incomes support you both in the styles to which you are accustomed?*
- *Are you both well-adjusted individuals?*
- *Have you agreed on your hopes and dreams for the future and on a basic life plan for your years together?*
- *Do your children, close friends, and family members support your decision to marry? If not, how can you address their disapproval?*
- *Can you talk comfortably together about your previous mate without making comparisons?*[39]

Another danger of moving too quickly, particularly for an elderly, lonely woman, is that of fraud. One must accept the adage that "If it

---

[39] Think of Your Future, AARP Workbook, (New York: Harper Collins 1995) p 78

sounds too good to be true, it probably is." Stories abound of women who have had their assets stolen from them because they trusted a convincing, loving man who professed his fidelity and devotion. And then, as soon as she had given access to her bank accounts, he disappeared--with her money--and the remainder of her faith and trust.

And, let's face it, it's exponentially more difficult for an older widow to find someone her own age, because the males of her age are usually looking for younger, more attractive wives. The younger woman excites the libido of the older man, and the older man can provide material security to the younger woman (that a man her own age cannot). The older, more mature widow often gets left out of the equation.

Remember that in a great many instances, even two years is not enough time to let go of one relationship and start another. Even though having that other special person in your life can bring particular warmth and comfort, if the expectations brought into the new marriage are too high and are not realistic, there can be many disappointments and unhappiness—not what you had planned for going into a new union.

WHEN WILL IT BE DONE?

So--how long is grieving supposed to take? As long as it takes. There is no "fast-forward" button. The process of grieving differs from person to person. Don't let anyone else tell you how to grieve or how long it's supposed to take.

Towards the end of her life Dr. Kubler-Ross extended her stages of *Death and Dying* into those of *Grief and Grieving*. The advancement of these original five stages promoted a new profession of psychologists and counselors, dedicated to easing the grief-stricken through the grieving process.

But Kubler-Ross had based her stages of grieving on her personal observations of a *dying* person—not a grieving person. And newer and fresher research done by others called to question her hypothesis. The new findings suggested that the Kubler-Ross stages were no longer valid; however, the grieving person still needed to be actively involved throughout the grieving process through a series of phases, tasks, or needs.

Additional researchers, however, using newer and more sophisticated models for collecting data, have shown that it is not necessarily more beneficial that the grieving person be required to "work" through the grief process, but that the different stages will come and go, back and forth, and *eventually* will lift.

In her book, *The Year of Magical Thinking*, Joan Didion says: "Grief has no distance. Grief comes in waves, paroxysms, sudden apprehensions that weaken the knees and blind the eyes and obliterate the dailiness [sic] of life. Virtually everyone who has ever experienced grief mentions this phenomenon of 'waves'."[40]

Some days you will be strong and looking to the future, and some days you will be crumpled into a ball wanting to die. Everyone copes with their grief on their own timetable--and in their own way. You can't expect the end of grieving to come by a certain time. You can't make the end of grieving happen. The new research says that while we know that loss is forever, acute grief is not--and it will end.

After Gary died it took me a long time to listen to the tapes of his history that he had dictated in those last weeks. I finally hired other people to transcribe them for me so I wouldn't have to listen to his voice. But eventually I had to put everything together, edit, clean out duplications, and put it all in order.

The end result is an historical, picture-filled, printed, bound book, copies of which I have given to our children and to interested family members. It is a tribute to Gary and to his life but, equally as important, a cathartic letting go for me. Compiling his history was a strategic coping mechanism for me, as has been writing this book.

Another way of coping that provided me with the most consolation and reassurance has been for me to write letters to Gary. My journal entries have fallen off as I have recounted my life's happenings in letters to him. I can pour out my heart detailing my miseries and successes and those of our children. It creates a connection that is more profound than I can describe!

What has worked for me will, in all likelihood, not provide the same type of comfort for anyone else. Each person comes through grieving in his or her own best way.

Life goes on, and with the passage of time the loneliness begins to subside and the sorrow from painful memories diminishes.

---

[40] Didion, p 27

Looking back is replaced with looking forward. The future is bright and full of promise and hope.

Author, Catherine Sanders says: "The real strength of grief comes from a new, if slowly arriving, self-awareness. We change without realizing it. Faced with few other options, we square our chin and reluctantly learn to deal with the situation on hand. We can see new alternatives opening up and we hold the freedom to choose. When we accept the freedom to select a way that is entirely our own, amazing things can happen."[41]

I am different—I am not the same person I was. I can't be. But my brain is healthy and productive, and even though I might be thought of as being "over-the-hill", I am still changing as I discover new things about myself.

Knowing of death is what gives life its meaning. I now know that life is precarious and short—and I don't want to waste a minute of it. I am learning about living and enjoying life in the moment—rather than the future or the past. My goal for each day is to do something that satisfies me, helps someone else, and justifies the reasons I am here.

I AM ALIVE. I have survived one of the most horrendous experiences life holds in store for us. I have survived the ultimate abandonment. I have survived the slings and arrows. And I am resolved to be the stronger for it.

I am often asked, "Does it ever get better?" My answer is, "No, it just gets different."

---

[41] Sanders, p 106

A NEW DAY

Each new day God gives us a brand new world. What can I do, just
   today, to make my new world better than it was yesterday?
I will be happy and bring happiness to those who are around me by
   sharing a smile or a happy word.
I will not weep or spread sorrow--even when the depressive burden
   encompasses my heart.
I will do something, however small, for another person to ease that
   person's day--keeping a promise, bringing a laugh, lifting a spirit.
I will love my God better, remembering to daily include Him in my
   thoughts and plans.
I will use my productive mind--helping to create and build a new and
   better world for tomorrow---
And then--I will begin the next new day in my brand new—and
   better—world.

KRP – June 2012

APPENDIX

If possible, gather all the paper information into a separate notebook or file box. If it is not convenient (or safe) to keep the paperwork in the same files, make a note of the location of the papers. Remember that this information, all together, is extremely valuable to anyone who would find it, so keep it safe and secure. If your files are paper, put them behind lock and key. If the information is collected electronically, transfer it to a flash drive or CD, store in a safe deposit box, and delete the information from your computer.

CHAPTER ONE—PRINCE, PAUPER OR SCULLERY MAID

Gather financial information in a separate notebook or computer file. For each of the following make note of (1) the name, address and phone number of the company (or financial institution); (2) the account numbers; (3) balances in the accounts; (4) location of the papers; and (5) name and phone number of agent or representative, if any:

MONEY ON DEPOSIT

    Pension/Retirement Funds – from where?

    Savings and checking

        Is there a secret savings account somewhere?

    IRA Accounts

        Investments

Stocks, Bonds
    US Government Bonds
Other certificates of investments
        Name, address and phone number of stock broker
        Certificates of Deposit
Annuities
        Name, address and phone number of financial planner
Paid up real estate?
Cash – is it stashed away somewhere? If you don't want others
to know where it is, put the location of the cash in a sealed
envelope in the safe deposit box where it can be found on your
death.

LOANS
Reverse mortgage
    Loan balance
Residential mortgage
Loan balance
Second mortgage
    Loan balance
Credit card(s)
    Loan balance(s)
Automobile/ boats/ RVs – also get information on insurance
    policies
    Loan balance(s)
    Leases and car titles
Other loans; e.g., education, home improvement, etc.
    Loan balances

RENTAL INCOME
Names, addresses and phone numbers of tenants
Monthly lease payments to you

147

ANY ACCOUNTS RECEIVABLE (money owed to you)
   Copies of contracts

CHAPTER TWO

INSURANCE – Gather the following information on your term life, whole life, universal life, etc. insurance policies
   Name, address and phone number of company
   Name, address and phone number of agent
   Policy numbers and location of policies
   Names, addresses and phone numbers of the beneficiaries

LIVING TRUST and/or WILL (for both yourself and your spouse)
   Name, address and phone number of law office of attorney
   Name, address and phone number of attorney
   Location of Living Trust and/or Will
   Name, address and phone number of the executor of your estate
   Name, address and phone number of your tax prepare person

HEIRLOOMS
   List of heirlooms – where is each located?
   Method of distribution

CHAPTER THREE

All the items pertaining to this chapter are listed in the body of the chapter. Just make certain that the location of each item is noted.

CHAPTER FOUR

Paperwork for any funeral pre-planning you have done, or
Directions to survivors for your funeral
   Funeral home to be contacted
      Choice of casket
      Choice of clothes
      Choice of flowers
   Cremation desired?

Obituary
    What newspapers to use, what picture to use
    Name a charity in lieu of flowers (?)
Funeral service
    Location
    Who to conduct
    Speakers
    Music
    Pall bearers
Approximate price to be paid
Organ donor?
Name of cemetery – where do you want to be buried?
    Existing plot?
    Inscription to be on the marker.
    What about a veteran's marker?
Who should be notified of your death?

CHAPTER FIVE

Paperwork for the Advance Directive or the POLST – where is it?
    Location of the "Do Not Resuscitate" form (this should be in an
        obvious place)
Paperwork for Durable Power of Attorney for Healthcare –
    where is it?
Name and phone number of your Health Care Proxy aka Health
    Care Advocate
Driver's license indicating your desire to be an organ donor
Hospice care
    Name and phone number of attending caretaker

CHAPTER SIX

Final arrangements for immediately after the death:
    At least 12-15 death certificates

Sometimes the funeral home will take care of this. If not, you get them from the Health Department in your county or state. There is usually a small charge for this.

Social security benefits

Where is your Social Security card? You need birth and death certificates of the deceased, marriage and divorce (if applicable) certificate of the spouse, birth certificates of dependent children, Social Security numbers, and copies of the deceased's most recent federal income tax return.

Military records if the deceased is a veteran, particularly a certificate of honorable discharge.

What war/date, place of induction/date and place of discharge Branch of service

Contact local Veterans Administration office for help with burial expenses. It won't be much, but every little bit helps.

Copy of marriage certificate, if spouse is applying for benefits.

Copy of dependent children birth certificates.

Copy of all insurance policies.

Life insurance policies can be settled fairly quickly and money paid directly to the beneficiary(s).

Check all insurance policies—mortgage loan, accident, home, automobile

Copy of medical records

Copy of education records

Employee benefits

There may be survivor benefits from work.

Is there a final pay-check?

Workman's comp if the death was work-related.

There may be pension benefits for the surviving spouse from the company, union or professional membership.

Credit card – cancel all credit cards that are exclusively in the name of deceased. Any balance(s) due will be paid from the estate.

Taxes

> Federal estate tax – paid for estates that exceed $5,000,000
>
> State estate taxes
>
> Inheritance taxes – not every state requires an inheritance tax
>
> Income taxes – federal and state income taxes for the deceased are due for the year of the death.

Debts

> All debts owed by the deceased should be paid from the estate by the executor. Debts that are owed jointly by both spouses should be paid for by the survivor.

Change of ownership and/or title – For items that were held jointly by both spouses, the ownership will automatically transfer to the surviving spouse. Others may require some work.

> > Where are the deeds or titles to those items that are singly or jointly owned?
>
> If the deceased has not already signed the car title transferring ownership to the surviving spouse, take a death certificate and title of the car to the State Department that regulates motor vehicles.

Assets such as savings accounts, stocks and bonds, other investments—if these have not been transferred into a joint account of both spouses, the items will probably have to be probated.

Insurance policies

> Beneficiaries will need to be changed; coverage may need to be updated

Safe deposit box

> Location of the keys
>
> If box was rented only in the name of the deceased, the box may need to be drilled open in order to obtain materials pertaining to the death. Other items in the box will probably need to be probated.

Contracts
    Business agreements
    Copy of all contracts showing your obligations to others and their obligations to you.
        Are there any verbal or moral obligations to be upheld?

EVERYTHING ELSE (needing to be gathered)
    Emergency phone numbers.
    Names, addresses and phone numbers of:
        children and spouses, grandchildren and spouses
        important relatives
        important neighbors and friends
        business associates
    Passport
    Religious affiliation
    Names, addresses and phone numbers of memberships in professional organizations and in societal organizations
    List of employers and dates of service
    Citizenship papers
    Copies of last three years income tax returns
    Copies of last three years property tax receipts

Personal papers – if there is anything embarrassing or incriminating for either spouse, destroy the papers immediately—don't wait for them to fall into the wrong hands.

BIBLIOGRAPHY

Brothers, Joyce. <u>Widowed</u>. New York: Ballantine, 1990.

Block, Sandra. "Managing Your Money" <u>USA Today</u> 23 Oct. 2009.

Callanan, Maggie and Patricia Kelley. <u>Final Gifts</u>. New York: Bantam 1992.

Collins, Thomas. "Putting Your Papers in Order is First Job for Retirement" <u>Utah Retirement Systems</u> Oct. 98.

"Death: It's a Living" <u>CNBC TV Special Report</u> " 31 Jan. 2013.
"Death isn't just a certainty; it's an industry built around a set of rituals designed to ease grieving – and drive profits. Once bound by tradition, this highly competitive and little understood business is reinventing itself for the 21st century."

Didion, Joan. <u>The Year of Magical Thinking</u>. New York: Vintage, 2005.

Hargrave, Terry D. "Hard Questions" <u>Modern Maturity</u> AARP, May/June 2001.

Hoffman, Ellen. "When Couples Clam Up" <u>AARP Bulletin</u> June 2002.

Lloyd, Nancy. "Protect Your Heirs after You're Gone" <u>Parade Magazine</u> 25 Feb.2001.

<u>Making Health Care Decisions for Others: A Guide to Being a Health Care Proxy or Surrogate.</u>The Division of Bioethics, Montefiore Medical Center, Albert Einstein College of Medicine,Bronx, New York.

McLeod, Beth Witrogen. <u>Caregiving, the Spiritual Journey of Love, Loss, and Renewal.</u> New York: John Wiley & Sons 1999.

Oishi, Emily and Sue Thompson. <u>Before It's too Late—Don't Leave Your Loved Ones Unprepared</u>. United States n.p. 2000.

Parachin, Victor. "10 Common Myths & Realities about Grief" <u>The Director </u>March 1999 [the official publication of NFDA].

------------. "Grief Relief", <u>The Director</u> Aug. 2001.

Quinn, Jane Bryant. "Financially Speaking" <u>AARP Bulletin</u> March 2012.

Ranks, David. Personal conversation, 13 Sept. 2012. Ph.D., FACPN, Diplomate, American Board of Professional Neuropsychology.

Rasmusson, Erika and Janes Lisa Scherzer. "10 Things Funeral Directors Won't Tell You" <u>SmartMoney.com</u> 28 June 2010.

Reilly, John W. <u>The Language of Real Estate.</u> Chicago: Dearborn Financial Publishing 2000.

Sanburn, Josh. "The New American Way of Death" <u>Time Magazine</u> 24 June 2013

Sanders, Catherine M. <u>Surviving Grief</u>. New York: Wiley & Sons, Inc., 1992.

Sheehy, Gail. "The Secret Caregivers" <u>AARP Magazine</u> May 2010.

Staudacher, Carol. <u>A Time to Grieve</u>. New York: HarperCollins 1994.

<u>Think of Your Future, AARP Workbook</u>, New York: Harper Collins 1995.

Wheeler, Barbara R. <u>When a Spouse Dies</u>. Utah, Plain Sight Publishing 2012.

Whitesides, Robert, J.D. Personal conversations, Oct. 2012.

Williams, Elisa. "Handing It Down" <u>Better Homes & Gardens</u> Nov. 2004.

<u>www.archrespite.org</u>
<u>www.cancer.gov</u>
<u>www.caringinfo.org/i4a/pages/indes.dfm?pageid+3277</u>
   Advanced Care Planning information – state by state guide<u>www.cremationassociation.org/?page=WhatToAsk</u>
<u>www.diabetes.org</u>
<u>en.wikipedia.org/wiki/Elisabeth Kubler Ross</u>
<u>www.fivewishesonline.agingwithdignity.org</u>
<u>www.medicalinformation.org</u>
<u>www.medicare.gov/caregivers/paying for care</u>
<u>www.medicare.gov/pubs/pdf/02154,pdf</u>
   Medicare Hospice book
<u>www.medicinenet.com</u>
<u>www.myfico.com</u>
   for looking up FICO score. A score of 800-850 is ideal. Below 600 the borrower will pay higher points to borrow money.
   Equifax at 800-685-1111
   Experian at 888-397-3742
   Trans Union at 800-888-4213

www.National Alliance for Caregiving/AARP National Caregiver Survey 2003.

www.nfda.org/grief-resources/understanding-death.

www.nfda.org/media-center/statisticsreports.html
2010 NFDA General Price List Survey.

www.palliativedoctors.org
definition of Hospice

www.parents.com

www.seniorcareassociates.com
Veterans Aid and Attendance benefits

www.ssa.gov
Information on Social Security

www.time.com/time/magazine/article/ Konigsberg, Ruth Davis
"New Ways to Think About Grief" 29 Jan. 2011

www.yourturntocare.or

ABOUT THE AUTHOR

Karen Post has been a writer of just about anything and everything for the past sixty or more years. She has written books, courses, magazine articles, newsletters, minutes, notes to school, letters, and lots of email postings; but she has never before written a book on losing a spouse and the resulting consequences of trying to restructure a life as a different, but fulfilled, single person.

Karen graduated from the University of Utah in the field of Education and has spent her life teaching, writing and, hopefully, helping others in their own path.

Karen's very ethnic and wonderful family (including spouses), of whom she is extremely proud, consists of eleven Caucasian, one Chinese, four Vietnamese, one black, and two adorable mixed-race great-grandchildren. And one very curious, trouble-making dog.

5284716R00097

Made in the USA
San Bernardino, CA
01 November 2013